MW00576126

ALASKA
NOME
IDITAROD
FLAT
FAIRBANKS
MOUNT MCKINLEY Natl. Park
KATMAI Natl. Mon.
ANCHORAGE
DAWSON
WHITEHORSE
CANADA
GLACIER BAY Natl. Mon.
JUNEAU
SITKA
PRINCE RUPERT
ALASKA HWY
MARINE HWY
SEATTLE
BENNETT
Canada
U.S.
Chilkoot Pass
White Pass
DYEA
SKAGWAY
Lynn Canal

"Bound for Dawson;" twenty-one men from Norman , Silvana and the greater Stanwood area in front of the Hotel Northern in Seattle, WA preparing to leave for the Klondike Gold Rush in the spring of 1899. The *Seattle Daily Times*, February 17, 1899, reported J. B. Lee, J T. Wagness and E. O. Anderson, who have been identified in this photograph, staying at the Hotel Northern along with Ed Wagness, E. O. Foss. Andrew Larson, O. Prestlien, O. Larson and A. Larken.
Photograph by John T. Wagness
Stanwood Area Historical Society #2004.16.03

To Seek the Smiles of Dame Fortune

Stanwood Tales of the Last Great Gold Rush

by Richard A. Hanks

Coyote Hill Press
2022

Published by Coyote Hill Press, Camano Island, WA

Layout & Design by Robin S. Hanks

First Edition, 2022

Printed in the United States

ISBN: 978-1-7358615-5-5

Front Cover: "Bound for Dawson;" twenty-one men from Norman , Silvana and the greater Stanwood area in front of the Hotel Northern in Seattle, WA preparing to leave for the Klondike Gold Rush in the spring of 1899. The *Seattle Daily Times*, February 17, 1899, reported J. B. Lee, J T. Wagness and E. O. Anderson, who have been identified in this photograph, staying at the Hotel Northern along with Ed Wagness, E. O. Foss. Andrew Larson, O. Prestlien, O. Larson and A. Larken. Photograph by John T. Wagness Stanwood Area Historical Society #2004.16.03

Contents

Acknowledgements

Words can nourish the heart but photographs help us peek into the soul. Together they work to expand the meaning of any content or message. I am grateful for the assistance of the following people and their institutions for providing images for this work.

Thank you.

Karen Prasse--Stanwood Area Historical Society.

Ruba Sadi--University of Washington Special Collecton.

Sandra Johnston--Alaska State Library.

Aurora San Miguel--Museum of History and Industry.

Preface

The story of the Yukon gold rush of 1897 - 1899 and subsequent strikes which followed around Alaska is not just about men seeking wealth but more the question as to why men, or women, leave everything they know and risk the travails of the wilderness for the slimmest of hopes that there is something at the end of an imagined rainbow. The American artist Thomas Hart Benton wrote that people such as these were "the most hilariously hopeful people imaginable…the mere fact that they were off somewhere gave them an immense vitality." That vitality was created by staring into the unknown and believing that the future held something greater for themselves. The unknown has a way of drawing people in because the fears of consequences or successes are cloaked in the hopeful feelings of what could be. Benton wrote that "they move on the wildest hearsay that for many results in more hardship and more violent and dangerous battles for mere food and shelter than would ever have been known had they rested content in familiar localities."[1] But it is such decisions that change the human condition.

Most of the fifteen men and one woman chronicled in this work did not achieve the pinnacle of the hopes they held dear and may be looked upon as mere anecdotes in the larger scheme of history and the era in which they lived. But, for their very real everyday lives they advanced the possibilities of the world to which they were born. What was unapparent at the time, but manifest later, was that their attempts, their labors for something better, benefited the community in which they lived even without their understanding and even if it did not elevate substantially their own lives. Progress, whether personal or larger, is incremental. What often seems just a moment in time in historical review, is often the movement of change on a grander scale. Such it was for the men who brought their wealth, whether great or small, and their experiences back with them from the frozen north to the small town along the shores of the Stillaguamish River where they lived out their days.

These were common men with uncommon aspirations often born from the hardship of the surroundings that accompanied the times in which they lived. Young farmers, loggers or budding entrepreneurs, their stories mirror the desires of many but only attempted by the few. So it was in the raw and difficult gold fields of the Yukon and Alaska. Many attempted that path but few actually found even a modicum of accomplishment. Their goals were not lofty, but very mundane—a better life and freedom from the plagues of poverty and uncertainty.

British officer and archaeologist T.E. Lawrence wrote that, "All men dream: but not equally. Those who dream by night in the dusty recesses of their minds wake in the day to find that it was vanity: but the dreamers of the day are dangerous men, for they may act their dreams with open eyes, to make it possible."[2]

This book is dedicated to those few dreamers who persevered and reached for what seemed remote if not impossible.

Richard A. Hanks

Henry Anderson's "river of gold"

Henry Anderson and John P. Anderson

On July 17, 1897 Captain William Kidston eased the steamer *Portland* aside Seattle's Schwabacher's Dock as five thousand excited people crowded the waterfront to cheer its arrival. News of the *Portland's* golden cargo had already spread like wildfire through Seattle; the news being rapidly relayed after the

Wilhelm Hester, Steamer Portland, ca. 1900,
University of Washington Special Collections, Hester 10609

steamer *Excelsior* docked two days earlier in San Francisco with a similar consignment. Estimates of the wealth onboard varied from $700,000 to a million dollars of gold nugget and dust—"STACKS OF YELLOW METAL," shouted the *Post-Intelligencer.*[3] Over a ton of Klondike riches was reported. Historian Pierre Berton wrote that street cars stopped running as operators quit and mass resignations hit all sectors including clerks, police officers, reporters and doctors, disrupting life in the city. Gold fever, however, lifted the hard times that plagued Seattle following the panic of 1893. "Prosperity is here," declared the *Post-Intelligencer* soon after the ship's arrival.[4] The arrival of the *Portland* created the stampede which would see thousands rush north for the precious metal.

Reporters clamored onto the ship eager to talk with the 68 proprietors of northern wealth. Most miners were eager to boast of their new found fortunes, all except one man, Henry Anderson.[5] According to the *Seattle Daily Times*, Anderson "refused to talk, hurrying aft to get away, but it was said by his companions that he brought down $65,000, and that he had a claim like a river of gold. He sold out a half interest for $45,000. In six hours shoveling he secured 1,025 ounces from his claim."[6] That would be the first of Anderson's golden acquisitions. His acquired wealth would, in years ahead, raise the financial status and security of the small logging and shipping haven of Stanwood, Washington situated between Port Susan and Skagit Bay.

Henry Christian Anderson's circuitous route to the Klondike goldfields began in Norway where he was born sometime between 1865 and 1867. He traveled

Henry C. Anderson
Illustrated History of Skagit and Snohomish Counties, 1906

with his widowed mother Madli to America around the year 1868 living for a time in Kansas, Texas and Colorado. In 1887 he and his mother moved to Stanwood, Washington to live with her sister Anna Maria Gjertsdatter Lindebrekke Leque, wife of Nels Paeter Leque. Henry worked for this uncle as did good friend and fellow Norwegian John P. (Johan Peter) Anderson who came to Stanwood at about the same time. Henry left farm work for a time becoming a clerk in a commission house in Seattle in 1889 before returning to farm work in Stanwood.

John.P. Anderson, ca. 1900
Stanwood Area Historical Society #2021.23.15

In June 1895, Henry, joined by J. P., "resolved to seek the smiles of Dame Fortune." Both traveled to the newly built Fort Cudahy in Canada's Northwest Territory where they found employment with the North American Trading and Transportation Company. Henry was manager and head salesman of the company.[7] The fort was across from the community of Fortymile at the confluence of the Yukon and Fortymile Rivers. The town, said to be the oldest in the Yukon, was founded in 1886 after gold was discovered in the area—the first stampede town. Fortymile City is roughly 48 miles downriver from where Dawson City in Canada's Yukon Territory would emerge ten years later after discovery of its own golden plenty. Writer A. J. Roan wrote that "by 1894, Forty Mile boasted two well-equipped stores, ACC [Alaska Commercial Company] and the North American Transportation and Trading Company, a lending library, billiard room, 10 saloons, two restaurants, a theatre, an opera house, a watchmaker, and numerous distilleries." By 1895, when Henry and J. P. Anderson boarded the *Willapa* steamer in Seattle for Alaska, over $400,000 worth of gold had been extracted from the Fortymile region. Roughly a thousand people were living there at the time.[8]

Henry and John (J. P.) Anderson were perfectly situated when George Carmack walked into Bill McPhee's Saloon in August of 1896 announcing the gold strike he and his partners, Skookum Jim and Tagish Charley made on the Yukon's Rabbit Creek, a claim he was there to record. Carmack renamed the waterway of his strike Bonanza Creek which was a tributary of the Klondike River. "Lying George," as he was nicknamed, was initially laughed off but news spread and miners, including Henry and J.P. Anderson, quickly abandoned Fortymile City

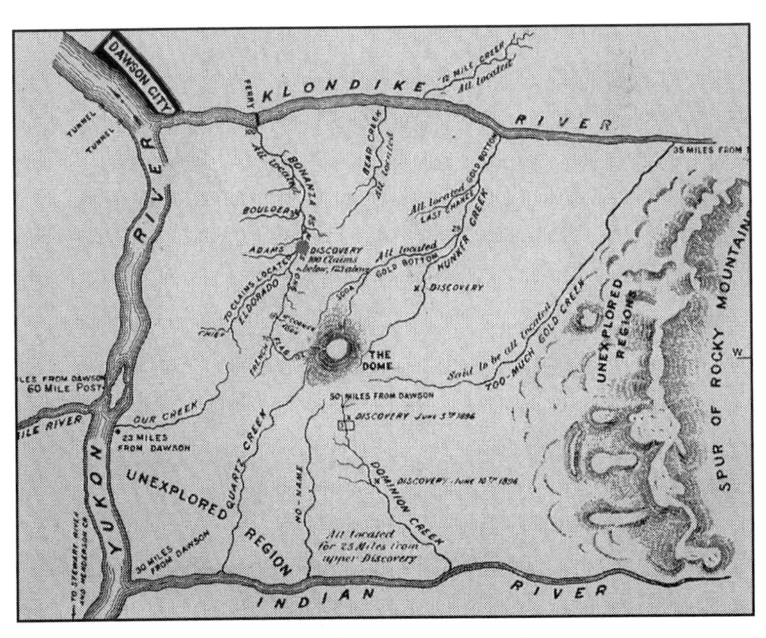

Klondike Gold Rush Map, Wikimedia Commons

which was essentially deserted by the winter of 1896-97.[9] Both men reportedly laid claim to rich lodes; Henry filing on Eldorado #32, a creek which fed into Bonanza, which he worked with partners William Sloan and D. L. Spencer. Dawson at that time was a brutal and crude settlement of the naïve and hopeful. Historian Berton wrote of Dawson that "no other community on earth had a greater percentage of potential millionaires, yet all its citizens were living under worse condition of squalor than any sharecropper. Food was so scarce that all but the most expensive dogs had to be killed because the owners did not have enough to feed them."[10] Sloan was also aboard the *Portland* when it docked in July 1897. The *Post-Intelligencer* wrote that Sloan was a former dry goods merchant from Nanaimo, British Columbia who sold out his interest for $62,000 and "has come back to civilization."[11]

J. P. laid claim to #42 along Bonanza Creek itself. He made a go of this operation until 1906 when he returned to Stanwood and invested his riches in "valuable farms" many of which he leased to others and from which he derived a "substantial income." He is credited with incorporating the first dredge into Klondike mining in August 1901. By the end of 1899, many adventurers to the Yukon had either given up finding riches or moved on to other gold strikes in Alaska in particular. By the summer of 1901 those who stayed were crying for more efficient ways of extracting the remaining pay dirt from the often frozen earth. J. P. Anderson secured the dredge from the Lewis River Mining and Dredging Company and had the massive superstructure floated down river to Dawson. It took weeks to move the machinery up

Dredging operations at Bonanza Creek, Yukon Territory, ca, 1900,
Museum of History and Industry, shs7258

Bonanza Creek and put it in place, afloat in a large man-made dam.

The *Daily Morning Alaskan* newspaper described the operation: "The earth is dug from the creek bottom with a series of heavy and sharpfaced iron buckets on an endless chain swung about on a great crane. The buckets gouge out the earth beneath the water and roll up at an increasing angle that hold the contents until finally they are spilled and fall into sluice boxes running over the hull of the plant. Water flows through the sluices continually and the process of washing the ever falling buckets of earth is continuous." Anderson reportedly paid $250,000

John and Jennie Anderson, February 11, 1903
Stanwood Area Historical Society #93.21.04

for the equipment, a sign of the success he had found along that creek bed at that time. Three eight-hour shifts ran day and night to keep the operation moving.[12]

J. P. Anderson married Jennie Ryan of Stanwood on February 11, 1903. He wrote to his new bride after returning to his claim the following year. "I

E.A. Hegg, Front Street, Dawson, Yukon Territory, June 1898
University of Washington Collections, Hegg400, from Wikimedia Commons

am ground sluicing as hard as I can and I have two men working both shifts and catching a little sleep whenever I can. The Yukon River broke [ice] in front of Dawson April 10 but it only moved about a mile and stopped and did not move again until the 13th. The first steamboat arrived yesterday…and I expect my baggage have arrived about this time. The first steamers left for Fairbanks yesterday, but it had only about 40 passengers. I am trying to work a big cut this summer and will employ about 16 men when I get ready to take out pay dirt which will be about June 10. I went to Dawson yesterday and bought my lumber for pump and waterwheel and I met Ivar Floe there. He said that everything was all right with the family and he said he intended to stay over on Quartz Creek until he have [sic] made his fortune."[13]

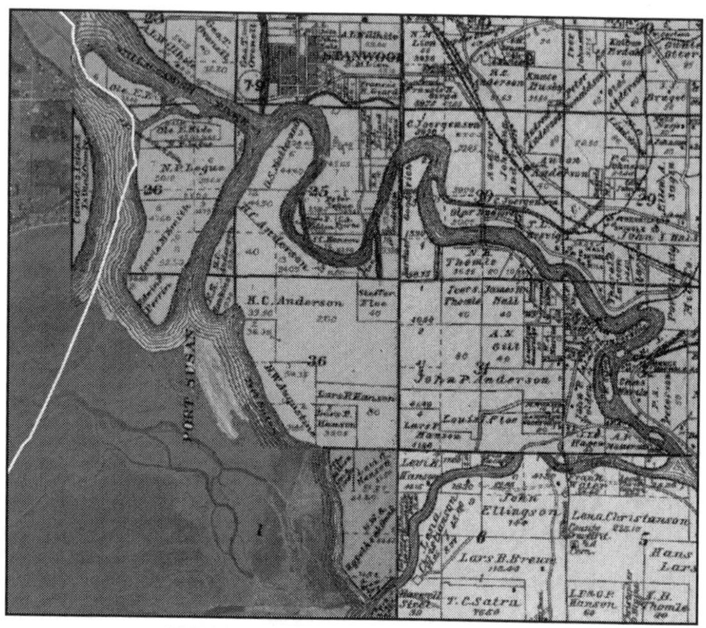

1910 Map of Florence Island, Washington
http://www.gfhistory.org/Maps.html

John Anderson returned to the Stanwood area in 1906, although he continued to lease his Klondike operation to others. He invested his northern earnings in land, purchasing several properties, one where he bred pure Holstein cattle. Anderson died in November 1938. He was a fervent member of the Masons and enjoyed the "unqualified esteem of all with whom he has been associated."[14]

Henry Anderson, who would earn the moniker of "Klondike Charlie" in later years, would also put his money into land and cattle but his other holdings were extensive throughout the Puget Sound. In 1898, 33-year-old Henry Anderson bought 400 acres on Florence Island south of Stanwood. After clearing the land, he pastured it with Durham and later Holstein cattle. In July of that year the *Seattle Daily Times* reported that Henry had "brought out" $175,000 in gold dust. The paper added that Henry and his partners, Spencer and Sloan, had disposed of their claim on Eldorado #32 before they left Dawson City. Another resident of Stanwood, John B. Lee, bought half of that claim around this time.[15]

Like J. P., Henry and partners were still getting payment for the claims sold or leased. On August 13, 1899 Henry arrived with M. Knudson at Seattle on the steamer *Humboldt*, this time with a reported cargo of 400 pounds of dust worth thousands of dollars. They wasted no time in moving the dust to the assayer's office and then to the Cherry Street hill smelter; not Henry's "first pilgrimage" according to the paper. Henry was still booking steamer passage to Juneau as late as February 1914, the same year he died.[16] By 1900 He was diversifying his land holdings around the Puget Sound including buying two large ranches in Skagit County and the Peterson Dairy farm in Roy, just south of Tacoma and properties within Stanwood. In February of 1901, he bought a three-story brick building in Seattle for $40,000 cash on the Isaac Parker block. Anderson initiated the organization of the First Bank of Stanwood which opened on August 4, 1904 with a capitalization of $25,000—all local money. Anderson was president, Peter Leque (his brother-in-law as well as first cousin) was vice-president, W. C. Brokaw and S. A. Thompson were cashier and assistant cashier respectively. Alfred Densmore and Francis Giard were trustees. Stanwood could now boast, wrote Alice Essex, "one of the finest banking institutions in the county." He was a major investor in the H & H Railroad, the one mile rail line which connected the mills of the western waterfront with the Great Northern depot east of Stanwood. In 1912, he bought an interest in the Northwestern Woodenware Company of Tacoma for $75,000. Henry was a long-term member of the Yukon Order of Pioneers, Seattle Lodge No. 2. Membership was for "all white men who were on the watershed of the Yukon River before July 1, 1899." The order's inception began in December of 1894 at Snow's Opera House in Fortymile. Henry arrived a year later. One of the other Seattle members was George Carmack, who with his two partners first discovered gold in 1896 initiating the Klondike stampede.[17]

Henry Anderson found love later in life but it would be accompanied by as much heartache. Brother-in-law Peter Leque drowned in 1905 prompting Ida Iverson to leave her studies at Mark Hopkins Institute in San Francisco and rush home to console her sister Bertha, Peter's wife. Their meeting at this time led to the marriage of Henry and Ida on June 24, 1906 in Thurston County. By then Ida was teaching at Garfield school in Olympia after graduating from Bellingham Normal school.[18]

It was likely during 1912 that the Anderson family met nurse Miss June Oakes, an advocate of Linda Barfield Hazzard, the so-called "starvation doctor" who promoted long-term fasting as a way to combat disease and find better health. Reportedly Oakes was first hired by Henry to help him recover from ptomaine poisoning. Oakes impressed Ida who then brought her back into the home to help care for daughter Agnes Madli (nicknamed Goody) born in February 1911 and newborn son Robert Anderson

The Wedding of Ida Iverson and Henry C. "Klondike" Anderson
on June 24, 1906 at the home of O.B. Iverson in Olympia, Washington
Stanwood Area Historical Society #2003.05.01

born October 11, 1912. Tragically, the infant lived barely a month before dying November 12th which some report was exacerbated by mud baths given by Oakes to the infant. By December of that year, however, both Henry and his mother Madli became concerned that Agnes was becoming malnourished under Oakes' supervision and the fasting regimen she prescribed for the child. Dr. Donald McEacheran of Stanwood was notified on December 30th of the problem.

Through the demands of McEacheran, Henry and Grandma Anderson, the girl was given a wholesome meal while they observed. This was done despite the opposition of Ida and nurse Oakes. The next day Oakes and Ida Anderson took Agnes and left Stanwood on the train without letting Henry know. Henry hired a Pinkerton detective to track them

Agnes Anderson, ca. 1911
Stanwood Area Historical Society #93.21.06

down and after several days they were located in Tacoma. Agnes was said to be in an emaciated condition—"on the point of starvation." After a few days of proper food, the little girl and Ida were removed to the home of R. J. McLaughlin in Seattle, friends of the Andersons. Oakes, however, resumed visitations to Agnes and with Ida's support began again the controversial fasting leading to another intervention and efforts to remove Agnes from Ida's control. This time Ida's mother Maria Iverson took the child to her Stanwood home to nurse it back to good health. At that time Grandmother Iverson told the local newspaper: "When I saw the child with its mother in Seattle the skin was stretched tightly over the bone of its little fingers, for there was no flesh on it, and the little ribs fairly protruded from the body. At the Mclaughlin home I thought the child was gone,

I lifted it from its bed, held it in my arms for some time before I could see if it still had the breath of life, and when I saw a slight breathing I was again hopeful that its life might be spared."

Ida was first removed to Providence Hospital before going to University Hospital, a private institution and finally Raleigh Hotel where she had shared apartments with her sister Bertha three years earlier. Here she began again her communication with Oakes as well as Hazzard telling her brother F. A. Iverson that she was only dieting, not fasting. Henry, who had his own apartments in Seattle's Butler Hotel, frequently called upon his wife. The last time was March 19, 1913 where he found Ida "apparently in good health, but thin." Plans were made for Ida to return to her home in Stanwood. However, early on March 20th Henry was called by Butterworths Undertaking Parlors and told that Ida had died. She died at 5 a.m. after summoning nurse Oakes to her bedside.[19]

Henry and Ida's family demanded prosecutors convene a coroner's inquest to investigate Ida's death. The obvious answer determined by the jury, after 10 minutes of deliberation, was death by starvation. Dr. Louis Rubenstein testified that he found an unusual quantity of alum, an astringent, in Ida's stomach meant to shrivel the stomach lining, reducing feelings of hunger. Oakes did not notify the coroner, a doctor, the hotel or relatives upon Ida's death and instead had the body embalmed two days before the coroner was notified, a point of irritation for Rubenstein. Oakes testified that she left Stanwood with Ida "to protect Mrs. Anderson from the ignorance of her relatives." When asked what she thought was the cause of Ida's death she responded: "I believe she died of grief." Oakes volunteered unproven hearsay that Ida and Henry were having trouble at home and hinted at abusive treatment. After taking the stand, Hazzard claimed she never encouraged Ida to fast and that treatments of Ida had only been osteopathic and at her request.[20]

Ironically Linda Hazzard had already been convicted of manslaughter in January of 1912 for the starvation death of British heiress Claire Williamson at her sanitarium Wilderness Heights in Kitsap County. Her medical license had been revoked by the time of Ida's inquest. For Williamson's death she was sentenced to two to twenty years in prison which was upheld on appeal. She finally served two years of that sentence in the penitentiary at Walla Walla, Washington but she was paroled December 26, 1915. She was given a full pardon by Governor Ernest Lister a year later. She would undergo her own fasting cure in 1938 and die of starvation.[21]

Perhaps it was a way of luring Ida to return home or just Henry Anderson's overt expression of his wealth and fortune, when he purchased 51 acres on a west-facing bluff overlooking the Stillaguamish Valley and his holdings with a commanding view of Stanwood, Camano and Whidbey Islands along with the Olympic mountains. An architect designed the 7,140 square-foot modified craftsman-style home with its colonnades and large portico protecting the entrance off a curved driveway.

The finest hardwoods from the east were used for the downstairs with clear fir upstairs and cedar roof shingles. Henry personally inspected the materials and oversaw the construction. The house was adorned with indoor window boxes that drained to the outside and beveled stained glass windows. Upstairs five bedrooms radiated from the large landing at the top of the stairs which reporter Peggy Wendel described as "a room in itself with enough space for furniture between bedroom doorways," and in between the bedrooms was a screened-in sleeping porch.

Linda Burfield Hazzard, Wikipedia

The home was finished in the spring of 1914, a year after the death of Ida Anderson. Henry lost his mother Madli less than a month after Ida's death. He tried to numb his sorrow with liquor which only worsened his health. He died of chronic gastritis and a weakened heart on August 6, 1914 at the age of 49. Reportedly it was Anderson's wish that his daughter Goody be raised by his business partner and friend Clyde Brokaw and the Brokaw family moved into the mansion to take care of the girl. However, it is more likely that W. C. Brokaw, Clyde's father, was the initial guardian of Goody. After he died in 1920, Clyde would have assumed that role. Bill Brokaw, his son, was born a year later. Goody was 10 years old when Bill was born—"she was like a sister to me," he remembered. Goody was "pretty well fixed, said

Brokaw, "she could do what she wanted as long as she could talk my dad into it. He was pretty strict with her."

Goody Anderson attended an exclusive girls' school in Tacoma (the Annie Wright School) and would travel the world by ship and air in later years. She owned an apartment building in Seattle and leased out the Skagit and Snohomish farms her father owned. Agnes Anderson married twice; the first time to Joseph Greenough who wooed her when she was attending Mills College in Tacoma and married Agnes in 1933. In 1945 she married John Nash Ott and moved to Winnetka, Illinois. She and John retired to Sarasota, Florida in 1967. Agnes passed in 1982. She had five sons, one by Greenough, and four by Ott.

Henry C. Anderson's legacy is the financial stability he brought to Stanwood through the riches he found in the Klondike. That wealth, however, did not provide the happiness he might have imagined. He lived just a few months in his mansion, paid for by his serendipitous wealth, which represented his hope for the future.[22]

The Mining Man & the Photo Artist

John B. Lee and John T. Wagness

Sketch of John Lee, *Klondike Nuggett*, Nov 1, 1899

John B. Lee reportedly went to Fortymile in the same year of 1895 as J.P. and Henry Anderson. Lee was born in Otter Tail County, Minnesota in March 1869. His family moved to Tacoma in 1887 where he was employed by the Northern Pacific Railroad as a boiler-maker. As the economy worsened in the early 1890s, Lee leased a farm in the area of Norman, Washington, southeast of Stanwood. When the lease expired in 1895, he headed for the gold fields. This decision may have inspired a similar effort by another former resident of Otter Tail,who also moved to Norman, Bernard Estby, who ran a successful drilling operation in the Yukon and Alaska.

An 1899 profile of John said that he then "came on" to the Dawson area when the 1896 stampede

Sluicing operation run by John Lee, *Klondike Nugget,* November 1, 1899

happened a year later. The article started with an admonition for those who might try but not have the fortitude to do the work needed to brave the perils of seeking the golden ore from the unforgiving landscape. "The hardship and dangers that men have undergone in reaching the Yukon gold fields can never be realistically portrayed on paper. They can be appreciated only by the man who has been there. To understand it all requires the actual experience. It requires that the man who would know what hardship is should take his pack on his back and climb the Chilcoot [sic] summit in the midst of blinding blizzards."[23]

Sluicing Operation , Photograph by John Wagness, ca. 1898
Stanwood Area Historical Society #95.03.57

As previously mentioned, Lee purchased a half interest in the Klondike's lucrative Eldorado #32 and owned two other interests, one on Sulphur below #32 and No. 4 on Gay Gulch. By the time of the profile Lee had married Lillian DeVoe (or Devasse) in Dawson on July 1, 1898 and adopted her daughter Olive. They lived on their Eldorado property where John actively supervised the work. Lee had a large operation employing 24 workers running day and night shifts. A newspaper touted him as a "mining man of a number of years' experience" who quickly saw the need to improve ways of working the frozen ground. Lee implemented a steam plant which thawed the ground and was used to hoist dirt and pumped water into a massive sluicing operation. The paper noted that Lee is "essentially a modest man,

Photograph at Dawson City by John Wagness. Man on far left may be John Lee.
Stanwood Area Historical Society SAHS #95.03.55. ca. 1900

who dislikes notoriety of any kind. He prefers to enjoy the results of his success in the Yukon in quiet without the spectacular accompaniment of sensational newspaper displays. He is an open-hearted and generous friend, to which fact many who have been the recipients of his acts of kindness can testify."[24]

Despite owning part of Eldorado #32, it doesn't appear that he acquired the wealth that graced Henry Anderson but it was enough for John to buy 133 acres around Norman in 1898. Family history believes that Lee lost, re-made and lost a fortune in gold including mining ventures back in the states, particularly in Colorado. In fact, Lee died in Denver in January of 1928. It was Lee's initial success which prompted him to write to his brother-in-law, Tacoma photographer John T. Wagness, urging Wagness to join him in the

John B. Lee standing with sister Clara Lee behind John & Mary Lee Wagness
Stanwood Area Historical Society #95.03.14. ca. 1900

northern gold fields. John Wagness' daughter-in-law told a reporter in 1997 that from letters and research they believe that John Lee wanted Wagness to chronicle Lee's mining achievement in pictures. Lee was "stalwart in frame, with the hearty and brusque manner of an adventurous frontiersman..."[25]

Wagness, whose original name was Johann Thorvold Vikness was born in Ulvik, Norway in 1857. After his family's immigration in 1872, they settled in Fergus Falls, Minnesota. By 1880 Vikness (Wagness) was living in Fargo, Dakota Territory and working as a "photo artist" as stated in the 1880 census. A year later the Fargo city directory shows him running a confectionery. It is believed that the John Wigness [sic], part of the partnership of Wigness and Foseide, who operated a studio in Fargo in 1886, is likely the same John Wagness described here.[26] It is probable that the Wagness family and Lee family were familiar with each other since the Lees lived a few miles away from Fergus Falls in a village named Tordenskjold by 1870. Reportedly, Mary Lee, was born in Fergus Falls in 1868. She married John T. Wagness on November 25, 1889 in Tacoma, WA.

Both the Wagness and Lee families are shown living in the Seattle/Tacoma area by 1887. That year Wagness "of Fargo, Dakota," became an associate of photographer C. E. King. They opened the new Sunbeam Gallery on June 15, 1887 at the corner of 11th and Pacific Ave. in Tacoma. By November of that same year, Wagness purchased the shop from King. Fires, however, plagued his endeavors to succeed. Considerable damage was done to his gallery on January 9, 1890. Immediate estimates deemed the building irreparable. The building housed a bakery, pawn brokerage and real estate office besides Wagness' studio on the upper floor. Assessments placed the start of the blaze in Wagness' studio sparked by spontaneous combustion of chemicals used in his photography. Despite the setback, a month later Wagness announced his re-opened shop

John B. Lee (left) and brother-in-law, John T. Wagness, ca. 1900
Stanwood Area Historical Society #95.03.26

E.A. Hegg, Broadway St., Skagway, Alaska, May 20, 1898,
University of Washington Special Collections, Hegg 20A

at the same location, as "most superior to the old, making it the most complete gallery in Tacoma." On February 23, 1890 the building amazingly caught fire again, this time emanating from the Tacoma bakery. Wagness regrouped again and was open within a month advertising pricing on cabinet cards at the same location. He soon moved his studio, however, to 121 S. 11th Street.[27]

In 1891 his studio was praised as the "leading one for fine work….In fine portraits and views he has no equal." He had seven employees "constantly employed," stated a Tacoma paper. That studio was sold to Lynn and Lindahl in November of 1891. His new studio was at 947 C Street which was also damaged by fire in 1895 after the flames moved from a steam dye works in an adjoining building. He then relocated to 1128 Pacific Ave. in 1897 and 1898 when he was contacted by Lee.[28]

Wagness heeded the call of his brother-in- law and readied his trip to the rugged north. Besides food and clothing there was also the burdensome equipment of an early 19th century photographer: bulky camera, heavy glass negatives and the chemicals needed to develop those images. He loaded all of this aboard the SS *Humboldt* in the spring of 1899, which took him to Dyea, Alaska where he prepared for the most arduous part of his journey, climbing Chilkoot Pass. Wagness' route to the Klondike was more cost effective if tremendously more strenuous. Dubbed the "poor man's route," Chilkoot was a shorter trek than nearby White Pass out of Skagway but a much steeper climb to reach the headwaters of the Yukon River at a chain of lakes in Yukon territory including Lake Bennett, Crater Lake and Lake Lindeman. Weather was not the only consideration for stampeders. The towns of Dyea and Skagway had "sunk into cesspools of crime and rackets, ruled by 'Soapy Smith' and his mob," according to writer Ross Anderson. Authorities were either "toothless or on Smith's payroll." Gunfire was said to be commonplace and con men and saloons seemed to populate every corner of particularly Skagway.

Chilkoot Pass climbs between 28 and 33 miles from sea level at Dyea to Lake Bennett. By 1898 the Canadian custom officials had posts at the top of the pass to collect levies and ensure that every miner had sufficient supplies to sustain them through a rough winter; everything from rolled oats to woolen socks in what amounted to nearly a ton. For Wagness that

E. A Hegg, Miners climb Chilkoot Pass, Sept. 1898,
Library and Archives Canada, C-005142, from Wikimedia Commons

included large glass negatives, printing solutions and photo emulsions which were not only poisonous but possibly explosive. Chilkoot first rose 900 feet to a place called the Scales where supplies could be stored if necessary and packs adjusted for the remaining climb which was roughly another 1,000 feet over steep, treacherous terrain. At this point 1,500 steps called the "Golden Stairs" had been cut into the ice to aid the laborious ascent permitting a single file line of travelers up the mountain, if you paid the toll. Many made the trip several times in order to haul all the required equipment to the top as did Wagness. At the summit he signed the required records of the Canadian Mounted Police with a sense

Photograph at Lake Bennett by John T. Wagness, ca. 1900
Stanwood Area Historical Society #95.03.54

of accomplishment: "March 22, 1899 WAGNESS, J. T. Norman, WA." Wagness spent a year in the Klondike producing iconic images of the places and people who struggled to find the financial cushion for their demanding lives. His son Ken said that the pictures-- the black and white images of the unkempt miners, aproned merchants and raw lifestyle of the stampeders, male and female—those were "his father's missing Eldorado."[29]

Wagness' return to Washington also meant a new home for his family. They left Tacoma for Stanwood in 1900. Getting a foothold in a new town took imagination and initiative. The 1904 city directory for Stanwood showed Wagness running a saloon and photography studio. The business index in 1905

John T. Wagness
Stanwood Area Historical Society #92.08.01.02

showed his operation featuring cigars and liquors. By 1906, however, photography was his only business. He would build a reputation over time as the seminal photographer of the Stanwood community's growth into the 20th century. John Wagness died in Stanwood on May 30, 1936. One 1900 history declared Wagness a genial photographer who "has gained the standing among the people as a man of ingenuity in his chosen profession."[30]

Beardless Boys and Dreamers

Agnes Deans Cameron,
Wikipedia, ca. 1885

It is estimated that 100,000 people set out for the Klondike between the years 1897 and 1899 but only between 30,000 and 40,000 reached their goal and of those, roughly 4,000 actually found gold to some degree. Hopefuls from as many as 40 different nations made the trek. Agnes Dean Cameron, educator, writer and adventurer passed through gold country in 1908 and remarked on what she saw:

The news of the strike on Yukon fields flashed round the world on wires invisible and visible, passed by word of mouth from chum to chum, and by moccasin telegraph was carried to remotest corners of the continent. Gold-fever is a disease without diagnosis or doctor—infectious, contagious, and hereditary; if its germ once stirs in a man's blood, till the day of his death

> he is not immune from an attack. The discovery of gold-dust in Dawson sent swarming through the waterways of sub-Arctic Canada a heterogeneous horde,—gamblers of a hundred hells, old-time miners from quiet firesides, beardless boys from their books, human parasites of two continents, and dreamers from the Seven Seas.[31]

Other dreamers from Stanwood who took the same harrowing trip as Wagness include Peter Henning, Francis Giard, James Esary, George Ovenell, William Gunderson, Dan McDonald and Andrew Olson. These men would have been considered cheechako, Chinook jargon for greenhorn newcomers to the task of seducing the precious ore from the raw surroundings of the Yukon. Over time experience might gain them the status of sourdoughs, or grizzled veterans of the north, named after the bread dough which was the staple of many a prospector.

George Ovenell and William Gunderson

George Ovenell made the trek in 1897 through Chilkoot at the age of 20. Although a farmer in the Stanwood area at the time, mining was not unknown to the Ovenell family. His father Theodore, also referred to as Thomas, reportedly left his home in England at the age of 13 and stowed away on a ship bound for California where he participated as a '49er during the California gold rush. After a short stay in Nova Scotia, Theodore returned to Whidbey Island in 1851 becoming one of the earliest homesteads in

George Ovenell, his sister Alice Ovenell Nutter and his mother Carrie Ovenell
Stanwood Area Historical Society #92.41.76

that country. After a failed marriage on Whidbey, Theodore came to the Stanwood area in the early 1870s. There he married Caroline Mary Crane in 1876. George was born of this union on July 2, 1877. Theodore reportedly died in Sonoma County, California in 1884. His widowed mother took George to Denver, where he was educated in common schools and attended the state university and a private military academy. George returned to Stanwood in 1896 and a year later got the gold fever. At the time of George's assault up Chilkoot an avalanche broke over the climbers covering the pass and several of the stampeders. Ovenell is credited with helping to dig out the prospectors buried in the slide. Upon his return home in 1898, he continued working the 122 acres purchased by his father in 1882 and expanded its operation. In 1907 he purchased the land from his mother.

On October 17, 1901 he married Martha Gunderson. Three years later Ovenell and Martha's brother William made a return journey to the gold fields, staying for a year. William and Martha were the progeny of another Norwegian pioneer, Peter Gunderson, who immigrated with his family in 1866. The family farmed in Minnesota and later South Dakota. Peter's father and mother died in the Midwest and he moved his family to Snohomish County in 1876 where his son William was born on March 17, 1884. Peter purchased 80 acres north of the town on land that was partially diked; an effort he continued. William was educated in local public schools and attended Parkland College in Tacoma. Afterwards he learned the butcher trade and was manager of the Silvana Trading Union. Neither Ovenell nor Gunderson appear to have had the luck of Charlie Anderson and returned to the agricultural pursuits they had left behind. Ovenell and Gunderson would specialize in dairy operations with Ovenell having a retail milk business in Stanwood. Gunderson was a member of the Snohomish Dairymen's Association and ran a butcher business in Stanwood until 1911. William Gunderson died in August 1917; George Ovenell in April 1922.[32]

James Esary

The Esary name would become synonymous with Camano Island logging in the latter 19th and early 20th centuries, but at the time James made his excursion up the passes to the Yukon in 1898 he was a bicycling agent in Seattle with a taste for opportunity. He sailed on the steamer *City of Seattle* on January 26, 1898. His task was to explore the trails up Chilkoot and White Pass for a company with a patented machine to extract frost from gold bearing gravel. He was accompanied by Frank Barron and Willis Thorp. Thorp was the more experienced of the trio and credited as being the first in 1896 to drive cattle from Alaska to the Yukon by way of the valley of the Chilkat River northwest of Skagway. At Fort Selkirk, Yukon Territory they floated the cattle downstream to Dawson City.

James D. Esary from Esary family data, Ancestry.com

The 246-mile route proved the most successful for getting herds to the north country despite thick timber and bad swamps. Thorp had a contentious opinion about the legality of Canadian Mounties collecting custom duties from those Americans entering their territory. After bringing 30 head of cattle to his butchering business at Lake Bennett in November 1897, he was approached by a Canadian inspector who charged Thorp $16 a head for each steer. Thorp protested, challenging Canadian authority, arguing that Lake Bennett was on American soil and not within Canadian jurisdiction. In

E. A. Hegg, White-Pass-Summit, March-1899, National Park Service, Klondike Gold Rush National Historical Park, George & Edna Rapuzzi Collection, KLGO 59624a.

February 1898 the Canadian Minister of the Interior ordered customs posts built at the summits of both Chilkoot and White Passes and Mounties began collecting duties on stampeders including those camping around lakes Bennett and Lindeman.[33]

A reporter for the *Seattle Post-Intelligencer* came upon the group and solicited their evaluation of the situation with duties, the passes and present conditions. Esary said that they first ventured up White Pass with 5,400 pounds of supplies on four large Yukon sleighs and two smaller 30-inch bob sleds (one for their dogs). They were pulled by four oxen. The trail was narrow and dangerous for sleds wider than 20 inches in many spots. Reaching

E. A. Hegg, Lake Bennett, B.C., ca. 1898,
University of Washington Special Collections, Hegg 2144A

Cutoff Canyon, the trail became steeper and they abandoned one sleigh. White Pass hotel was a welcome sight for weary travelers. The large log structure accommodated 60 people who slept three to a bed for 75 cents a night—blankets furnished by the customer. Meals were also 75 cents. "Comfortable? Well, I should say!" Esary volunteered. "There is no reluctance to sleeping three in a bunk in that climate." Frequently, Esary said, every bunk was filled and people slept on the floors and tables, whatever was available.

They resumed their steep climb to the summit of White Pass and remarked on "humorous incidents" such as an outfit hauling whisky until one of their

G. G. Murdock, Scales area, and Golden Stairs in Chilkoot Pass (on the left) showing overhead tramways, 1898, Library and Archives Canada, C004492, from Wikimedia Commons

horse teams slipped, hurling horse, man and sled "rolling down the bank to the snow drifts at the bottom." This was not the only episode of someone getting too close to the edge. Such incidents were the cause of White Pass becoming known as "Dead Horse Trail." After reaching the summit, Thorp stayed at his business at Lake Bennett and Barron and Esary made a reverse trip down Chilkoot Pass with a gale like wind at their backs cutting through their clothing "like a knife." It did make for a "lively time sliding down the summit" to Sheep Camp about 12 miles above Dyea. Echoing his partner Thorp, Esary also complained that the Canadian customs' houses built at the summits encroached on the American side.

Collections of the duties began in February 1898. "I cannot well understand how the United States is to tolerate this occupancy by the British without ever so much as a 'by your leave' or notice of any sort." Esary reported that the resentment by the prospectors to the "invasion" of Canadian officials was intense. There was some talk at Sheep Camp of barging their way through the waiting Mounties but "cooler heads...prevailed."[34]

James Esary was the youngest brother in a large family of possibly eleven children. He was born in August of 1875 in Virginia. Brothers, David, Tom and Andy, were early adventurers to the Pacific Northwest, coming a generation after initial "boomers" in the 1850s rushed to exploit the vast resources of the untamed Northwest. David and Tom, born in the mid-1850s, were a generation older than their brothers including James the youngest male in the family. Yet, it would be James who became the force behind extensive shipping and logging operations that brought the famly influence and wealth. Their extended family had a large presence in Virginia's Russell and Washington Counties under the surname Necessary, including their father William Jennings Necessary and mother Nancy Stevens Necessary.

Following the lead of her older sons, Nancy Esary moved the rest of her family to Seattle around 1883, after the death of her husband. In the mid-to-latter 1890s, James found local fame for his bicycling prowess. His numerous racing successes earned him the nickname of "Cyclone;" the *Seattle Star* declaring in 1907 that James, for years, was the "crack bicycle rider of the Northwest." In 1897, before exploring the passes of Alaska and the Yukon, he worked as a "bicycle agent."[35]

Over the next 20 plus years (1900 - 1924), James' logging, shipping and ferry services, in partnership with master mariner Captain H. B. Lovejoy, operated under various corporate entities such as Esary Bros., Camano Land and Lumber Company, Camano Commercial Company, Island Transporation Company and synonymously the Island Navigation Company. By 1916 the Island Navigation Company was known as one of "the busiest steam navigation companies on the Sound." A Seattle newspaper reported that Esary, "devotes practically all of his time to shipping, yet like all true 'salts,' the more he sees of the water the more time he wants to spend on it..."

Designed by Lovejoy, the Island Transportation Company launched the steamers *Calista, Clatawa, Camano* and *Whidbey*. Esary's yacht *Dreamerie* was christened in November 1920. Another Lovejoy design before his death in August 1919, the *Dreamerie* was Lovejoy's last ship. James Esary died on Camano Island on November 16, 1947.[36]

Francis Giard

It is likely that the same trail used by Thorp to drive cattle to Dawson via the Chilkat River valley was used by Francis Giard in 1898. His son later recounted that his father "rounded up cattle with one milk cow...and took them to Seattle and loaded them on the steamer. At Skagway, Dad jumped the off the

Photo by John T. Wagness, Dawson City, Yukon Territory, ca 1898
Stanwood Area Historical Society #95.03.04

steamer and they swam ashore." He rounded them up on the beach and drove them overland to Dawson. Crossing some of the swollen rivers along the way was dangerous and Giard picked the strongest animals and hung onto their tails to make it across the fast-flowing waters. Upon reaching the gold camps, Giard found that the miners would pay almost anything for fresh milk.

The Giard family arrived at Utsalady on Camano Island in the fall of 1889 when Francis was a 17-year-old teenager having been born in Granite Falls, Minnesota on July 25, 1872. He received his early schooling in Cass County, Dakota Territory where the family relocated when Francis was six. The

Giards soon purchased a farm in the Florence area south of Stanwood. Francis helped his father work the land in the area until the reports of the northern stampede grabbed his interest.

Frances Giard, First Mayor of East Stanwood, 1922-1931
Stanwood Area Historical Society #88.06.190.02

On a subsequent trip after his 1898 excursion, Giard did make his way across the steep and treacherous Chilkoot Pass and had to make the numerous trips to move the mandated supplies up the daunting height to the tent cities surrounding the inland lakes. He lived in a cabin with a partner for a time 200 miles outside of Dawson and after being snowed in ran out of sourdough and salt. Giard was able to wound a grizzly bear who threatened the men, later falling down a cliff to its death. This unexpected windfall allowed Giard and his partner to live off the bear meat until the thaw came.

After one excursion, Giard continued downriver to the area near Nome in Alaska Territory and wintered in 1900 with Iñupiat Natives in their village of Cheenik (Ikalikhvig-myut) near the trading post of Golovnin Bay on the Seward Peninsula. After gold was discovered in 1898, Golovin became a supply-relay point for transport to the north. Giard displayed his manufactured skis and skates to the fascinated Iñupiat. He thrived on the hospitality they showed him. While with the Iñupiat, Giard collected a trove of bearskins and Native artifacts during his stay and sailed for Seattle with his collection only to have the steamer break up during a storm. Giard survived by floating on debris back to the beach but lost everything else.

Overall, Francis Giard made six trips to the Klondike and brought out on one occasion $25,000 in gold dust according to his son. He exchanged the dust at the mint in San Francisco and returned to Stanwood with a suitcase of American greenbacks. A Seattle newspaper made note of Giard's success in March 1901 during his stay at a local hotel, saying that he was heavily interested in Dawson. They wrote that he "came to the city last fall from the Klondike and then went East for a pleasure trip. He is now on his way back to the interior and will go in before the breaking of the ice. He brought one of the heaviest individual sacks which came into Seattle last summer." He lingered long enough, however, to marry Anna Isaacson in April of 1901. Anna would give birth to a son and daughter. Mother and daughter, however, died of tuberculosis in 1912.

After his last trip to the Klondike around 1904, he purchased 90 acres on the south side of what was then called Burnway, which ran between the eastern and western sections of Stanwood. He also joined with Henry Anderson to found the Bank of Stanwood in that year. He would continue on that board until shortly before his death. He began building his house on the eastside around 1905 and platted the town in 1906 of what would become East Stanwood. In 1912 Francis Giard married again to Sophia B. Husby who gave birth to Marcella and later Francis Jr. In 1922, with the incorporation of East Stanwood, Francis Giard became the first mayor of the town where he served for eleven years the first time; he would serve three terms. Francis Giard died in October of 1956. He was 84 years of age. He was described as a man always "looking toward the accomplishment of real, and practical good."[37]

Peter Henning

In 1897 Peter Henning also explored the dual passes of White and Chilkoot. Born in Bergsjo, Sweden in February 1863, Peter and his half-brother Johann joined their father in Minnesota where Peter worked in logging and was a laborer for the railroad and local farms. Johann, after work in Minnesota mines, worked his way across Canada to Washington Territory. He encouraged Peter to join him which he did early in 1888. He found similar work around Seattle. There were jobs building canals, in logging and the mills and in 1891 road building for the Lake Superior & Manitoba Railroad which was pushing

E. A. Hegg, Freight and supplies on waterfront, Dyea, Alaska, ca. 1898, University of Washington Special Collections, Hegg58, from Wikimedia Commons

a link through the cascades to connect with a line moving west from Minnesota. Promotions put Peter at the head of a crew of workers which completed the job in 1893. He wanted to "get ahead" and his earnings found their way into the local bank. The live hard, play hard of the loggers' camps did not appeal to the thrifty Peter. One biographer credits that to Peter Henning's strong morality learned through his Lutheran upbringing. "His distaste for the seamy side of life revealed itself in his round condemnation of the boomtown fleshpots that arose to massage the masculine libido: 'nothing but a place to get the money from the men: saloons, gambling dens and other vile places that goes with towns like that.'"

The frugal Henning could not escape the Panic of 1893, however. Mines shut down all over the west according to historian J. Kingston Pierce. Lumber interests were hurt when railroads curtailed shipments from the Pacific Northwest. "Three-quarters of the shingle plants operating in the state in 1893 had closed within two years. Poorhouses throughout Western Washington had to turn their occupants out into the streets," wrote Pierce. Author Archie Binns wrote of the era, that "...men who thought they knew about storms and how to weather them went over like straw men. And when they picked themselves up they were empty-handed."[38] Despite the challenges, necessity tied Henning to the logging business during this time and he was able to put together a small crew in 1894 which cut cedar at Mulkiteo used for shingle bolts as well as at Haller City and in 1895 near Hood Canal. With him at Hood Canal was another Swedish immigrant John Nordstrom who had recently arrived in the Seattle area.[39]

News of the gold strike in the Yukon gave Henning, as it did for many others, a way out. He sold his logging equipment and booked passage to Dyea, Alaska. There he found that the Dyea-Klondike Transportation Company was initiating an ambitious plan to build a narrow gauge tramroad utilizing mine cars from Dyea up to the Scales at the base of the Golden Stairs of Chilkoot. At that point an aerial tramway would be built to usher goods and people up over the pass. This was to compete with two similar trams, one called the Peterson Hoist and one built by Archie Burns which used horse power and later steam and gasoline to pull laden sleds up

Photo by John T. Wagness, Dawson City,Yukon Territory, ca 1898
Stanwood Area Historical Society #95.03.05

the last 600 feet. Henning capitalized on his road building experience, particularly with Washington state railroads, and made a successful bid on the first stage of the job. He and his crew cleared brush and removed boulders from the planned roadway. By December of 1897 his stage of the operation was complete. Peter paid his crew and headed south to Seattle with a better understanding of what were the needs of those who made their way to Dawson City and the rich lodes, and the tedious labor that surrounded it.[40]

In the spring of 1898 Henning returned to Dyea with 11 horses, parts for two wagons and 18 tons of feed, tools, oakum, nails, bagged sugar and green tomatoes. His pack train made its way to the pass and once over the pass to the tent city on the shores of Lake Bennett. After constructing a scow and hiring a Swedish guide, he moved his cargo down river to Dawson where eager and sometimes desperate miners paid the entrepreneur whatever he asked. The horses and wagons were sold and immediately used for hauling freight. Peter Henning would be a seasonal resident. In the spring he would be at Lake Bennett putting together new barges to transport his wares to the needy in Dawson although when typhoid hit the area he moved to Granville on Dominion Creek 60 miles up the Indian River and roughly 50 miles south of Dawson. There he built a portable sawmill—said to be the first--to supply lumber for the growing businesses and homes, plus cordwood and timber for shoring up the mines. There were harrowing adventures in his travels in and out of the Yukon which were ameliorated by 1900 when the railroad reached Whitehorse from Skagway.

Henning did not follow the next stampede to Nome with the discovery of gold on the peninsula of Alaska. The adventurous challenges of the northern country had taken their toll and Peter had money enough to visit his mother back in Sweden. Her son, whom she feared she would not see again, returned a rich man sharing his shiny gold nuggets among admiring relatives who held them in awe. His father had sought reconciliation with wife Margta Henning but returned with Peter to America in the summer of 1901. His father Per stayed in Minnesota but Peter returned to Washington. Peter had known Emma Yngve from his days around Cedarhome. He had worked with her father Eric during his early days logging around Pilchuck Creek. At the age of 33, Peter married Emma on November 15, 1902. They lost a daughter Hazel in July 1903 after the infant contracted the flu. Emma had been battling tuberculosis even before the couple married and Peter took her to a sanitarium in New Mexico. Returning home to Stanwood, he purchased 38 acres on a hill east of Stanwood for $2,000 with its panoramic view of the Sound. He dubbed the new home Henning's Park. At its base it straddled the rail line of the Great Northern Railroad which had established a station at Stanwood in 1891.[41] Emma died on December 5, 1905. Peter busied himself outfitting his new home and keeping contact with friends. He began using some of his profits to purchase property in nearby Everett.

The widower returned to Alaska in 1908 and bid approximately $80,000 on a road project from Haines, Alaska to the trading post at Wells roughly 23 miles to the northwest which ran along the Chilkat River into the area's interior. Carving out a roadway along the rocky shore of the river was dangerous and difficult work. Shaving formidable cliffs and removing obstacles still required boring into boulders and dynamiting sections. But by the end of October 1908 wagons were able to transport their goods along the road and it gave the Chilkat Tlingit Natives of the ancient village of Kluckwan, just south of Wells, their first glimpse of a wheeled vehicle. Before leaving again for Seattle, Henning was honored by the tribe for his accomplishment with the road; a road which gave them better access to the outside world. Reporter Monty Snow of the *Daily Alaskan* who was covering the road's progress, paused to note the festivities on the evening of October 16th. "The

Headmen of Chilkat Tribe, 1907, P39-0443
Alaska State Library, Case & Draper Photo Collection

guest of honor, Mr. Henning, was dressed in the latest approved fashion, a blue shirt, overalls, lumber jack boots and three weeks growth of whiskers." The village was said to have turned out "en masse." After formalities, the hostess Mary Ashamed-of-her-face invited all to adjourn to the pavilion for dancing and small talk. "The hall was artistically decorated, a beautiful effect being produced by hanging Hooligan-old lamps from between festoons of dog salmon....At 11:30 a sumptuous meal of smoked salmon, seaweed and cranberry jelly was served." Music was provided by Professor Nolay-Boys orchestra and Henning was serenaded by the Kluckwan Choral club, "composed of the most aristocratic dogs in Kluckwan." Mrs.

Blue Mud's gown was the sensation of the evening: "canary colored waist…green skirt and pink satin slippers, the whole costume beautifully draped with a red blanket." As people began to leave in the wee hours of October 17th, all declared that it was "the best time of their lives."[42]

Henning again made his way back to the states. In 1909 he became partners with two Vancouver contractors, Arthur and Russel Palmer, and the three soon began securing contracts for bridge and railroad construction in British Columbia along Fraser River. His obituary neatly summed up the volume of work Henning and the Palmers accomplished: "…the B.C. Electric Railway line from Abbotsford to Chilliwack… the Canby [sic] street bridge in Vancouver…street and car work in the same city, contracted to build 14 miles of line for the Canadian National [railway] from Hope to Yale and then constructed the 52-mile line across the summit of the Rockies that tied the Canadian National's east and west end construction projects together." He had as many as 2,000 men working for him during the project.[43]

At the same time, Henning maintained his ties to the greater Stanwood area, owning a farm in Silvana and in later years would acquire ranch lands in New Mexico and farm land in Minnesota, worked by others. In 1912 he had his property east of Stanwood platted and sold lots making him wealthy by the standards of the day. Two years later he purchased enough shares of stock to become a trustee of the board of the State Bank of East Stanwood and later its president. That same year he married 26-year-old Nannie Carolina Carlson, although almost twice her age, whose family had come to Stanwood in

Peter and Nannie Henning and their four children, ca. 1920
Stanwood Area Historical Society #88.06.127.04

1903. He was president of the Stevens Pass Highway Association and spent 20 years on the Cedarhome school board beginning in 1920. Henning became a Snohomish County Commissioner in 1921 serving until 1929 and leading the Commission in 1925. During that time he championed the efforts to extensively pave county roads. A diehard Republican, he ran for state senator at the age of 74 in 1937 but lost. Around this time, he also became president of the Everett Abstract and Title Company. He was diagnosed with prostate cancer in 1943 and died March 22, 1955 in an Everett hospital.[44]

Andrew B. Klaeboe

Like Peter Henning and John Wagness, the business of A. B. Klaeboe was more mining the miners rather than clawing the earth for its hidden riches. A druggist by training and trade, Klaeboe spent much of his time between Alaska and Washington state but paused long enough to become the second mayor of Stanwood from 1907 to 1909.

Klaeboe was born in Norway in February 1859 where he began his study of pharmacy at the age of 14. He continued learning his trade at the University of Christiana in today's Oslo. The family was originally Danish and in 1906 Klaeboe boasted of having a list of all members of the family stretching back to the 16th century. When he was 24 years old he migrated to the United States spending six months clerking in a drug store in Baldwin, Wisconsin. He then moved on working with Henry Thompson in Portland, North Dakota rising to manager of the firm of Roberts & Anderson before coming to Stanwood in 1888. His operation was only the second drug business in Snohomish County and the first for the town of Stanwood. He married Sarah Jacobsen on February 23, 1889.[45]

The discovery of gold in 1896 captured his adventurous spirit, as it did so many others, and he moved to Juneau, Alaska where he began the Occidental Pharmacy operating the business for three years until the great Yukon rush was played out. His fellow citizens of Juneau found Klaeboe a "pleasant, affable gentleman and his friends would be delighted for him to return to Alaska where such men as he are needed." His signature black derby, so ubiquitious

Andrew B. Klaeboe
Illustrated History of Skagit and Snohomish Counties, 1906

in his pictures on the streets of Stanwood, was even noted by an Alaskan newspaper. He wears a 7 5/8 black colored stiff hat when he wears one, reported the paper. "It is well taken care of and is kept well brushed."[46]

After returning to Seattle, however, the new gold finds around Nome, Alaska in 1898 again set Klaeboe into action. A reporter for the *Seattle Daily Intelligencer* recorded Klaeboe's excitement. "Fully twelve or fifteen residents of our little town and vicinity [Stanwood] are going to Cape Nome in the spring," Klaboe volunteered as he placed "some shining twenties" down at the offices of the Pacific Clipper line for his own passage to the new diggings. "Of course there are three or four times that many contemplating the trip, but all will not go," he added. "I expect to try the drug business at Nome City. I am going to take in a big stock of drugs. I went north in 1896 but got no further than Juneau, where I ran a drug store for over two years."

The topic then turned to the most well known and successful of Stanwood Klondikers, Henry Anderson. Klaeboe was asked whether Anderson was planning a new attempt to find more riches around Nome? "No," he asserted, "Henry got about $300,000 of Klondike gold. He has some rich farms and a handsome income, so why should he take chances in order to obtain more gold?" Klaeboe offered. The practical druggist continued: "There should be such a thing as a man getting enough and I guess Henry is satisfied."[47]

It doesn't appear that Klaeboe stayed long in Nome. By May 1901 he was back in Seattle doing considerable business with the intention of starting a drug store in Stanwood. If true, then he apparently closed his earlier store in the town before venturing to Alaska at the start of the gold rush. He incorporated his Klaeboe Drug Company in the spring of 1909 with a capitalization of $15,000. A year later he is

Andrew Klaeboe on the right in front of Klaeboe Drug Company, ca. 1910
Stanwood Area Historical Society #92.125.03

listed as living in Seattle and working as a druggist suggesting he was then splitting his time between the two cities. In December 1913 Klaeboe sold his Stanwood business to William L. Reeves of Mount Vernon and left Stanwood. The 1920 census shows him living with his married daughter Olga Hofstad in Seattle. Andrew Klaeboe died later that year in November 1920. His 1906 biography stated that he was "energetic, wide awake, progressive and public-spirited, and none stands higher than he in the esteem and regard of the people of the Stillaguamish Valley..."[48]

Andrew Olson

In 1891 Andrew Olson was only six when he began listening to the stories of sailor and adventurer Nils Lövgren in his hometown of Krokvag, Sweden. Lövgren had sailed the world's oceans and prospected for gold in Alaska and Siberia. Andrew dreamed of such a life for himself. His mother had died during Andrew's birth and his father discouraged such talk of leaving home. Reaching the age of 18 in 1903, however, Andrew, with $100 of his mother's estate, sailed for America where he made his way by train to Washington and his uncle's farm in the Cedarhome area east of Stanwood. Andrew soon found work in the shingle mill of Nicklason & Walters and worked his way up to foreman. His father Olof and his new wife and family joined Andrew in 1905 but soon relocated to Matsqui, British Columbia and Andrew joined them.

News accounts of the Yukon and Alaskan gold strikes still grabbed his attention. An introduction to mine owner David Strandberg, however, changed the course of Andrew's life. Strandberg's company needed miners at the Ester Creek holdings. The mine was roughly 13 miles east of Fairbanks. Reaching Valdez he had to make the rest of the 400 miles to Fairbanks on foot. The work once he arrived was hard going. The tools were pick, shovel and wheelbarrow but the pay of seven dollars a day plus room and board was good for the time. An accident in 1908 on a return trip to Washington required a convalescence of two years. By the time Andrew returned to Alaska in 1912 Strandberg had moved his operations to the creeks around Flat City northwest of Anchorage. In 1919 he paid a return visit to his homeland of Sweden and later Russia working on a collective farm and learning more about the mining industry. Back in Washington he met and married Frida Stromberg in December of 1924.[49]

Andrew found new opportunities after returning to Alaska and formed his own company with Tony Lindstrom and Axel Palmgren. In 1928 they bought rights on Happy Creek near Flat. With the help of half-brother Edward, the company expanded. However, in 1933 on a train trip from Anchorage to Seward he met Walter Culver and who excited Andrew's interest in the platinum mines around Goodnews Bay, 200 miles south of Flat. They worked together to secure many of the claims in the area and in 1935 the Goodnews Bay Mining company was incorporated. Andrew had also brought his now extensive knowledge of mining mechanization with him which had increased production in Flat and would do the same at Goodnews Bay. Olson's company extracted approximately 650,000 ounces of platinum in continuous operations from 1934 until November 1975. Writer Sarah Hurst wrote that in 1938 the Goodnews Bay Mining Company "was handling more than a million cubic yards of dirt in a season and more than a million dollars worth of platinum."[50]

The company maintained offices in the White Henry Stuart building in Seattle. In February 1938 he and Frida purchased a grand stucco and brick Tudor mansion on Queen Anne's Hill on West Prospect Street with a spectacular view of Elliott Bay. Soon after the attack on Pearl Harbor, Frida took ill. After a stay in the hospital, the diagnosis was stomach cancer. Frida Olson died in March 1942. Andrew's loneliness was only highlighted after that by the large but empty home on Prospect Street. He sold the house in July of 1945. He looked for a place away from the city—something rural with land. He drove back one day to the area which had originally provided the young Swede with the warmth and security of home. There just southeast of Stanwood, Andrew found what he was looking for and the property was for sale. On December 8, 1943, Andrew bought 240 acres in the community of Silvana for just over 21-thousand dollars.[51]

Andrew Olson
from *Platinum King* by
Jan Olof Lindstrom and Karen Olson

At dinner one evening while visiting his half-sister in Seattle he was introduced to Dee Dodge, a local dental hygienist who had once worked at Goodnews Bay in the 1930s. Dee was perhaps 30 years younger than the 60-year-old Olson but despite their age difference they began seeing each other. They were married in April 1945. The couple continued to split their time between Alaska and the mining operations and the farm in Silvana. Dee took ill in the early 1970s sparking the same fears that Andrew experienced years before. Dee Olson died at the age of 60 on March 9, 1972 and was buried in Stanwood.[52]

On his 90th birthday, Andrew Olson invited friends and relatives to the Silvana farm to celebrate with food and memorable stories. Andrew Olson died in his sleep at his farm on March 19, 1981 at the age of 95. His fascination with the mechanized inventions used to extract the precious ore from the earth continued in his later years. According to Hurst, "Olson saw and contributed to the technological advances of the 20th century....He made a great deal of money from his mining company," wrote Hurst, "but his real motivation in life was adventure."[53]

Dan McDonald

Dan McDonald would probably be better remembered as a worker of horses and a cement contractor in Stanwood rather than a Klondiker but like many before him, McDonald explored the mines of British Columbia and Alaska in his youth. McDonald's background is firmly rooted in the Scottish clan to which he belonged. The clans MacDonell and MacDonald dominated the Glengarry region of Ontario, Canada after settling there in 1784. The name of the county comes from the Scottish glen which was the homeland of the MacDonells. Dan's father Roderick was reportedly born in Glengarry, Ontario in 1829. Besides farming, Roderick also

Dan McDonald seated in front, July 4, 1885
Stanwood Area Historical Society #88.06.314.02

specialized in the raising of draft horses; a talent he would take with him after immigrating to Alpena, Michigan. Dan McDonald himself was either born in Glengarry between 1867 and 1870 or in Alpena since he provides both locations to enumerators on different census records. Regardless of the exact location of his birth, his upbringing took place in the

Sketch of the Fraternal Hall that appeared in a 1902 Stanwood Tidings newspaper by Mary Allen, the wife of Dr. O.R. Allen, who was an artist.

forests of Michigan where at the age of 15 he hired out to tend several dozen horses as a barn boy.[54]

In 1886 he made his way to Seattle and worked for a logging crew in nearby Redmond greasing the skidways with dogfish oil to smooth logs on their way to mills; a dirty job given to the lowest on the rung. Not surprisingly, McDonald stayed only two months in that position and soon found work again handling saddle horses for a Seattle doctor. After less than a year, however, McDonald moved to the Stanwood area and once more took up logging this time around Arlington until 1896 when the news of the silver camps of Sandon, British Columbia drew his attention. This time the work was not just unpleasant but dangerous setting explosive points for extraction of the ore, although the wages were high. Two years later McDonald headed for the Klondike where he filed on several claims on Gold Hill at the mouth of Eldorado Creek. He remained in the Yukon for two years.

Little is known of his time in the Yukon, but again he represents the many who sought the smiles of Dame Fortune only to settle for the adventure and marginal boost to their lives. He returned to Seattle in 1903 and, perhaps remembering who he saw or met during his time in Stanwood, he joined the family of an active Irish family of the area, the Tolins. Dan McDonald married Gertrude Tolin on November 25, 1903. The Tolin family patriarch was Edward Tolin who was born in New Brunswick, Canada and came to Stanwood in 1890 with the skills of a carpenter. By 1893 he was Chief Ranger of the Court of Stanwood, Ancient Order of Foresters of America who built the Fraternal Hall (and Opera House) which opened in February 1902. He retired from active business in 1900 and became the custodian of the Fraternal Hall. He served one year as the city marshal of Stanwood in 1907. In 1908, after the hall's purchase by the Independent Order of Odd Fellows, he became the hall manager. The families of Tolin, McDonald, McDougall, O'Melia, Hall, Hogan, Carlson and Callaghan, among others, would comprise the first Catholic congregation in Stanwood with worship taking place initially in homes of the Tolins, Hogans and O'Melias with Father P. Dubbel from the Tulalip Reservation conducting the services.[55]

After his marriage, it appears that Dan joined the other Tolin family business--saloons. Edward and his sons were quite active in providing a supply of liquor to the local loggers of the Stillaguamish Valley as well as throughout northern Washington and later British

Eagle Saloon in Silvana, ca. 1908
Stanwood Area Historical Society, #92.40a.17

Columbia. From roughly 1907 to 1909 McDonald ran the Eagle Saloon in nearby Silvana. Joseph Tolin was his chief bartender at that time. During that time he built two store buildings in Stanwood, which he leased, along with the purchase of seven house lots in the town although in 1910 he is still living in the Tolin household. It appears that McDonald took up farming and worked as a concrete contractor after 1910. It is notable that his first child Mary Kathleen was born August 22, 1911 which might account for his new occupation. His obituary stated that he would be "best known" as a builder of cement pavements and several paved streets throughout Stanwood—a "memorial" to his part in the development of the city. A Snohomish County history in 1926 wrote that McDonald "has ever exerted his influence in behalf of good roads and improved educational facilities and is widely recognized as one of the substantial, respected and representative citizens of his community." Dan McDonald died January 18, 1946.

The Heavyweight "Idol of Fairbanks"

Billy Bates

The main bout at the I.O.O.F. Hall in Stanwood that November evening in 1914 was not between rising stars or would be champions. Likely the opponents were loggers looking to pick up some extra cash. They were identified only as "Beckman of English Camp" and "Hokins of Chehalis." The "Smokers" as they were called, were amateur, unsanctioned "fistic carnivals"[56] for the entertainment of the primarily male audience which gathered, sharing companionship and escape from the day's labor all through the haze of tobacco smoke which gave the contests their slang handle. Given the printed exclamation in the fight's advertising that night, however, the real attraction was not so much the fight or its combatants but the bout's referee—"Billie [sic] Bates."[57] Bates's reputation in the fighting

SMOKER!!
SAT. EVE. NOV. 21st
. . . IN THE . . .
I. O. O. F. HALL
. . . MAIN BOUT . . .
BECKMAN vs HOKINS
OF ENGLISH CAMP OF CHEHALIS
GOOD PRELIMINARIES
Referee . . Billie Bates

Advertisement in the Stanwood Tidings, November 13, 1914

game was largely forged in the harsh, frozen north of Canada's frontier. At one point in his life, he was a prizefighting "comer" in the raw and raucous mining camps of the Yukon.

Bates had the face of a fighter—a chiseled roadmap of the hard hours spent in the ring. He had once been dubbed by sportswriters as "the budding bruiser," the "idol of Fairbanks," and even the "Champion of Alaska" in 1905 and 1906.[58] By the time of Stanwood's great Beckman/Hokins bout, however, he was a rancher living just north of the Stanwood city limits on diked tidal flats along a road known conversely as Pacific or "Low Land" Highway.

William Jonathan Bates was born December 2, 1874 in Stormont, Dundas and Glengarry United Counties, Ontario, Canada to Robert and Mary Ann Mooney Bates; same area as the MacDonald family home. Theirs was a large Irish family including brothers John Robert, Samuel Lindsey, Alexander Joseph, Gilbert David and sisters Martha and Effie Agnes. The family moved to the area of Walla Walla, Washington Territory sometime around 1883, staying for roughly five years before moving on to Stanwood. The oldest son, John Robert died in 1898 as his brothers were joining the trek for riches in the gold fields of the Klondike along with perhaps 50 other Stanwood citizens.

The Bates boys had their hands in mining for the next 20 years but brother Billy found greater initial opportunity using his hands against opposing prize fighters. During his hey-day, Billy Bates either faced or worked with some of the premiere boxers of the era: names such as Philadelphia Jack O'Brien,

Billy Bates
Seattle Daily Times,1905

Nick Burley, Frank Slavin, Jimmy Britt and Bob Fitzsimmons. Those years would be Billy Bates' brush with greatness.

Billy first journeyed to Alaska in 1896 just looking for work and was listed on the 1900 census for Nome, Alaska. He gave his hometown as Stanwood, Washington and although a transient, his occupation

Photo by John T. Wagness, Dawson City,Yukon Territory, July 11, 1899.
Monte Carlo Dance Hall & Opera House in the middle.
Stanwood Area Historical Society #95.03.19

is mining. He may have arrived first in the area but was soon joined by his brothers Samuel and Gilbert (Gilley) who were also intent on mining. That may have been Billy's initial plan as well since he was a partner of the Bates Bros. company. We don't know exactly when Billy decided to trade the placer pan and pick axe for the boxing ring but there were rumors that he had fought several times in Nome between 1900 and 1901.[59] Bates fought as a heavyweight with his size generally coming in around 190-200 pounds while flirting with six feet in height, and sometimes as a light heavyweight (175 pounds) after that class was created in 1903. He was a "stout" fellow according to records.

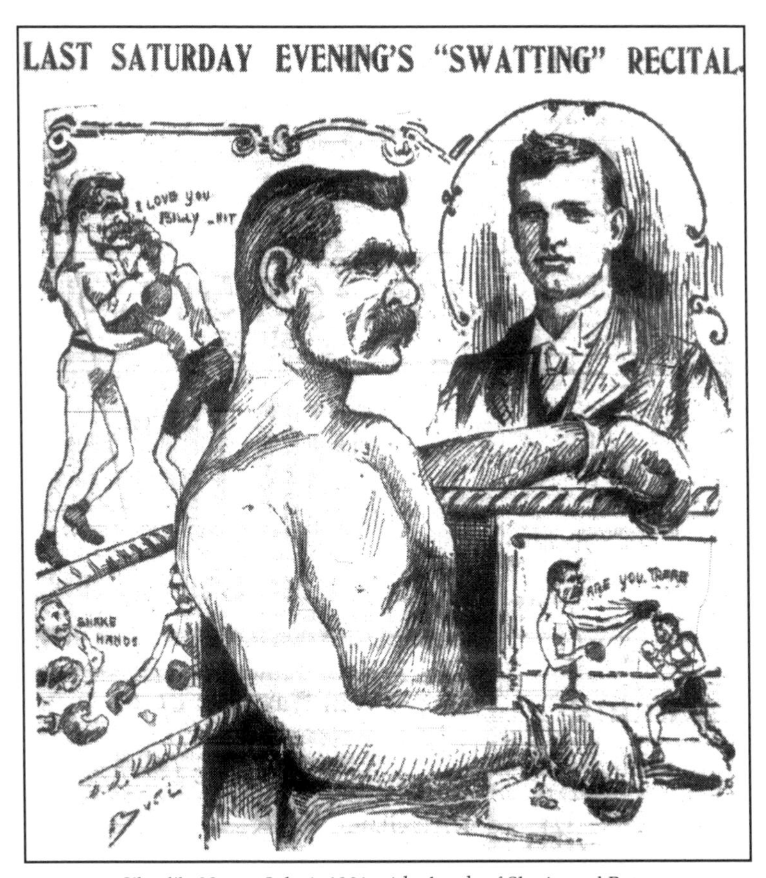
LAST SATURDAY EVENING'S "SWATTING" RECITAL.
SHAKE HANDS
ARE YOU THERE

Klondike Nugget July 1, 1901 with sketch of Slavin and Bates

One of his earliest recorded fights was against Australian heavyweight Frank Slavin, a former boxing champion of the world but a bit past his prime. The bout on June 29, 1901 was a "rattling good one" according to Dawson's paper. Bates, while doing most of the "manly work," got the worst of it, however. Slavin was the more persistent aggressor and many felt he should have the decision but was gracious when the call of a draw was announced.

Klondike Nugget September 3, 1901 with sketch of Perkins and Bates

Slavin came over to shake hands with Bates and complemented his "clever and vigorous work" in the ring and believed that Billy had a spendid future in the arena.[60]

The contest between Bates and Will Perkins on Sepember 6, 1901 at Dawson's Savoy Theatre was far less satisfying--a disappointment according to the *Klondike Nugget*. It lacked the science of skill or a test of strength. Perkins proved the agressor this time pursuing Bates around the ring with furious swings and jabs that largely missed Bates' defensive maneuvers. By the 10th round both men failed to land any effective blows. The outcome was another draw.[61]

Frank Gotch, Wikipedia, ca 1905

Boxers and wrestlers dominated the sports happenings in the early 1900s between Dawson City and Fairbanks, Alaska following the Klondike stampede and for Americans in general in the early 20th century. Wrestling historian Mike Chapman said that "at the turn of the 19th century in the early 1900s there were really only two sports that captured the imagination. It was boxing and wrestling." Other sports such as baseball, basketball and football were in their infancy, said Chapman. "The American male public really looked up to the combatant—the pugilist in sports—the heavyweight boxing championship of the world

Farmer Burns and Frank Gotch, Wikipedia, ca 1905

and the heavyweight wrestling championship of the world." One of those athletes was Frank Gotch, an Iowa farm boy turned professional wrestler, who came to Dawson City in the summer of 1901 along with manager Joe Carroll Marsh (aka Ole Marsh). None was more important to the wrestling game than Gotch, said Chapman. Gotch would go on to become wrestling's world heavyweight champion from 1908 to 1913 when he retired undefeated. According to Chapman, Gotch was for wrestling what Jim Thorpe was for football or Babe Ruth was for baseball—a "larger than life figure."[62]

After a couple of amateur fights in Iowa, Gotch caught the attention of Marsh and wrestler Farmer Burns who became his trainer. Historian Mark Hewitt wrote that Marsh and Gotch (using the name Frank Kennedy) went to the Klondike under Burn's direction and operated a "Badger Game;" a scam popular at that time in pro wrestling. Particularly in Dawson City, the pair orchestrated a series of challenges, including between each other, and contrived grudge matches which, over time, attracted growing crowds and excited wagering.

Journalist and photographer Tiv Kreling was a witness in 1900 to one of the Kennedy/Marsh bouts in Dawson City. Kreling was one of a team of reporters sent to the Yukon by the *San Francisco Examiner*. Marsh was taking all comers at the Monte Carlo Dance Hall and Opera House. Excitement hit a fever pitch after Gotch lasted the required 15 minutes with the boasting Marsh. A second single pin match was scheduled shortly afterwards. Tickets sold at premium prices and the contest stimulated heated betting. Kreling wrote that "you must remember that a bet of $1,000 meant but little more to those miners than a donation of $1 to the Red Cross means to us to-day. They would willingly give $2,000 or more to see a real wrestling match." Or, at least one that appeared to be real. After an hour and ten minutes, Gotch (Kennedy) was finally pinned and Kreling lost his wagered "poke" of gold dust but remembered that bout as "one of the greatest matches I ever saw or hope to see."[63] Billy Bates is not listed among the noted spectators that evening of the match, but he and Tiv Kreling became life-long friends as did Joe Carroll (aka Ole Marsh) who visited the Bates home in Stanwood in later years.[64]

The 24-year-old Gotch (as Kennedy) won several matches usually against local miners while in the Yukon and reportedly left the area $35,000 richer. Humboldt County, Iowa historian Jean Hinkle believed that Gotch was just going along for the ride. "A happy-go-lucky kid out on his own for the first time and enjoying every minute of the wrestling game."[65]

One of the more talked about matches was when Gotch tried his hand at boxing. Billy Bates was one of his corner men along with boxer Will Perkins. Gotch's opponent in Dawson City, Yukon Territory on September 25, 1901 was Frank Slavin. Perkins fought Slavin on July 10, 1900 and never fully recovered from the brutal beating which broke a rib and caused internal injuries. A fact which ended his life roughly six months after assisting Bates in the Gotch/Slavin matchup.[66]

Slavin later remembered meeting and arranging the match with Gotch to garner a bigger purse for both men. It was a packed house that night at Dawson's Savoy Theater. Slavin recalled that "the gathering in the theatre was picturesque in the extreme. Miners were there in their gumboots and furs, while some of the town folks put on their dress suits for old-time's sake. The patrons of the dance halls were there in their giddy attire. Outside the theatre dozens of dog

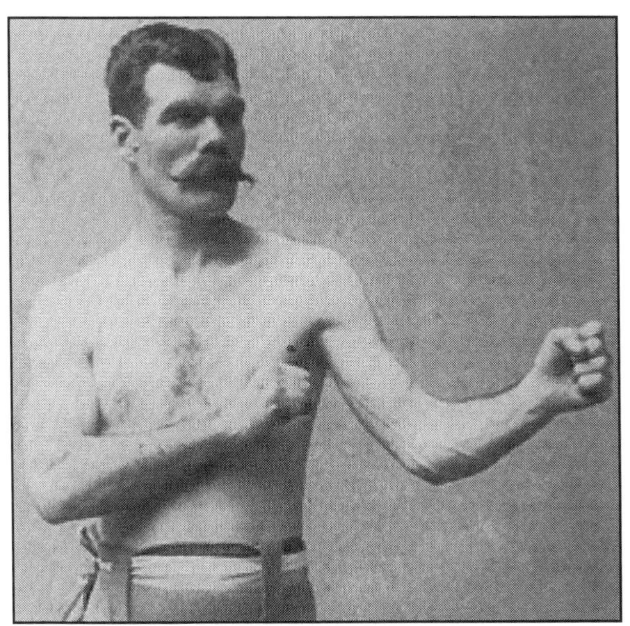

Frank Paddy Slavin, ca. 1900
boxing rec.com

teams were parked." Gotch was to take it slow so as to put on a show for the crowd but at the first sound of the gong he stormed out like a wild bull, swinging wildly at the maneuvering Slavin. "He kept on the aggressive," Slavin said, "and I cracked him with blow after blow as fast as I could get my gloves back. I shot more gloves at Gotch in the first round than I did at any other man in a dozen rounds." This continued until the fourth round with the nearly 40-year-old Slavin beginning to tire. He knew, however, "if one of his [Gotch's] vicious swings ever touched my chin I would be singing with the dickie birds." Gotch related the fight in 1907 telling the *Yukon World* that Slavin "must have hit at me fully 300 times in that scrap, and I didn't let one of the blows get by me. I stopped them all with my head or my body."

Frank Paddy Slavin, ca. 1900

By the fourth round, Gotch was becoming frustrated but determined. He told Bates and Perkins, "I ain't going to let this big dub knock me out." The bell rang and Gotch rushed out ducking under Slavin's ready guard and as Slavin recollected, "seized me by the waist, and picked me off the floor as easily as if I had been a child. Over his head I went and crashed through the ropes to the floor. I was bewildered." Slavin reportedly raised his head from the floor and asked "what kind of bloody fighting is this?" Referee Leroy Tozier asked if Slavin wanted to claim a foul? "Guess I'd better, or he'll throw me out into the audience next time," Slavin responded. In 1926 Slavin told an Australian newspaper that the match was the funniest of his career although a serious situation

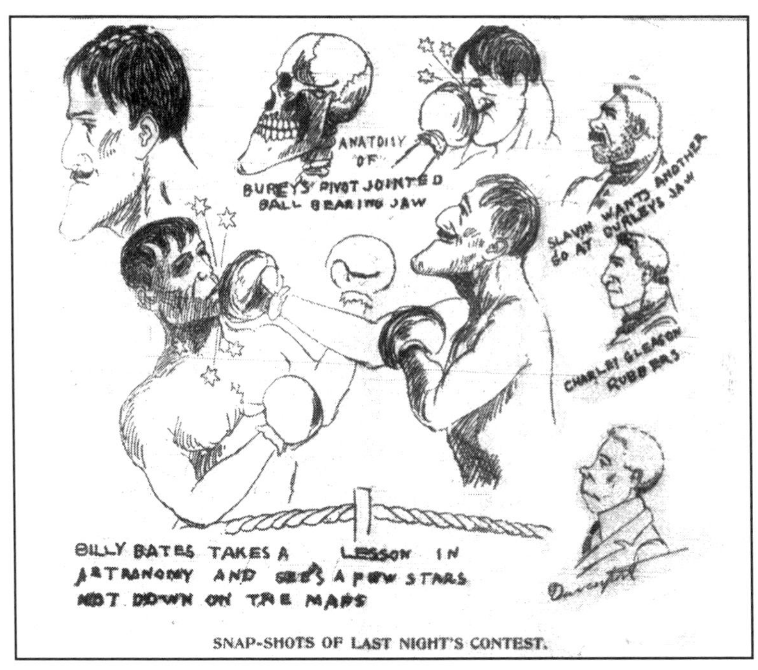

Klondike Nugget May 24, 1902 with sketch of Burley and Bates

while it lasted. Gotch stuck with wrestling after that.[67]

One of Bates' few recorded fights was against Nick Burley May 23, 1902 in Dawson City, Yukon Territory. Earlier that spring in April, Burley beat Slavin for the Heavyweight Championship of the Yukon. Burley had the match easily won by the third round when newspaper accounts say Bates fouled him. However, the crowd had so turned against Bates that Burley insisted the fight continue and the referee conceded to the demand. Despite Bates becoming "coarser and coarser in his fouls," Burley preceded to make his opponent a "chopping block" much to the delight of the boisterous, heated throng, before the ref called

Nick Burley from Findagrave, n.d. Posted by Carolyn Farnum.

the fight in the sixth round. Prolonging the fight was the correct action, said the paper, until Bates got the "knitting" he deserved. It was felt that Bates would never have a first class fight again after his performance.[68]

Bates obviously disagreed. Realizing he was outmatched by the talent in the Yukon, he traveled to San Francisco and enlisted the aid of one of the best boxing instructors of the time, Dewitt Van Court, who instructed Bates in some "fine points of the game" in preparation for the amateur boxing championship at the city's Olympic Auditorium. Trouble was that

Billy Bates was no longer an amateur. While there were rumors to that effect that made their way to newsprint, he entered the tournament, knocked out one challenger Louis Balletro in the second round and won the championship on a decision against the heavier 210-pound Andy Gallagher after a "fierce" three rounds. Bates was the "genuine surprise of the evening by giving…Gallagher a decisive beating," wrote the *San Francisco Chronicle*. Bates "learned the value of a straight punch in his first lessons, and it won for him over Gallagher's experience and generalship."[69]

With his win, however, came a number of witnesses with just as many stories about Bates' contests in the north. Some had seen his fight with Will Perkins as well as with Frank Slavin before his bout with Burley. Those two fights ended in a draw but in one he reportedly earned as much as $2,000 for his share of the purse. Bates never really offered a defense except to say that he considered himself a novice in the game who had only put on the gloves perhaps thirty times. He admitted the ten-rounder against Slavin but said he did not know the amateur rules and presumed that his previous actions had not jeopardized his standing. The tournament judges were unmoved and stripped Bates of his champion cup and expelled him from the amateur ranks.[70]

Now officially labeled a professional, Billy Bates hired out to work as a trainer for other fighters such as lightweight champion Jimmy Britt at his Oregon camp. Jimmy's brother Willie managed both fighters for a time. Bates also sparred with the lighter and smaller Britt in preparation for the lightweight's upcoming bout against Jack O'Keefe which also

Tiv Kreling on far left, Jimmy Britt fighter on left,
The *San Francisco Examiner,* January 23, 1940

ended in controversy. Britt retained his title but under a cloud since the fight was stopped in the sixth round when O'Keefe claimed an injury due to a foul by Britt.[71]

By July 1903 Bates was back in Dawson City where he reportedly stopped Montana heavyweight champion Ben Howard in the second round.[72] A good warmup for a re-match against the formidable Burley on September 28, 1903, again in Dawson City. The contest was said to have been lively from the start. The betting, not surprisingly, favored Burley. This fight was shorter than the first match but not much better for Billy Bates. News reports say that Burley put Bates "to sleep" in the third round.[73] Bates' friends complained that Billy was either doped or sick since they believed that "something was the matter with him."[74] This would not be the last time that Billy Bates attempted to even the score against the powerful Burley.

Roughly a year later Bates was again back on home ground in Washington, this time training a local favorite, Ches Levere, in Edmonds for a fight against Rufe Turner. Levere made more than one boxing appearance in Stanwood beginning in May of 1902 when he came out of retirement to fight "Indian Joe Gregg" to a draw. Stanwood's Fraternal Hall, also called the "Opera House," was the chosen boxing venue in that part of the upper Puget Sound starting in 1902 and well into the first two decades of the 20th century.[75]

Bates spoke to the press on Levere's behalf before a fight in Tacoma in the fall of 1904. "He knows it will be the making of him to win this battle and he is going out to do or die,"[76] Billy said. Unfortunately, Levere was "walloped…at will and punished…from coffee to cocktails" reported the *Seattle Daily Times*. Bates and others, wrote the paper, promised a faster, stronger and more scientific Levere. "If that is true, then Merciful Mayonaise! What was Levere in times past?" the paper added with notable disdain.[77]

After a year working and training with other prize fighters Billy was ready to have another go at Burley. Accounts of the July 3, 1905 fight are as few as the rounds fought. The *Yukon World* reported that Bates hit Burley with "a short arm jab in the ribs" and put the former Dawson champion "out of business."[78] In a letter released to the *Daily Alaska Dispatch* shortly after the fight, Burley grumbled to a friend that an injury had caused his loss. "I hit him [Bates] with my left hand and when I swung my right I broke my ankle in two places," Burley carped. "I dropped to the floor and could not get up." Burley was done with Fairbanks he said, complaining that he was heading for Nome at first chance. "This place [Fairbanks] is no good. No money or anything else." Bates, however, was now cheered as "ready to meet all comers."[79]

That next "comer" was Philadelphia Jack O'Brien. His reputation now resuscitated, Bates was granted a shot at one of the great light heavyweights of his era, whose real name was Joseph Francis Hagan. O'Brien and Slavin had been touring Alaska and the Yukon giving boxing exhibitions throughout the spring of 1905. The Bates/O'Brien bout was to be in late August of 1905 in Dawson City. O'Brien was eyeing the national championship after the retirement of Jim Jeffries and would face Bob Fitzsimmons for the title in December, just three months after fighting Bates.

O'Brien stood five feet ten and a half inches tall and ranged in weight between 152 and 165; an intelligent ring general with quick moves. He accepted challengers from any weight class while on his trip and that was to include heavyweight Bates who was reportedly 30 pounds heavier than O'Brien. This was undoubtedly a very important fight for Billy Bates. He had run the gauntlet of lesser-known heavy hitters in the various gold camps but O'Brien was a fighter of note. Bates and O'Brien entered the ring in Dawson City on August 30, 1905 for a ten-round bout. It would be a fight many remembered and long talked

Philadelphia Jack O'Brien, August 1911. Library of Congress
Prints and Photographs Div., LC-DIG-ggbain-09701

about, a true test for O'Brien and perhaps the zenith for Billy Bates' career.

Bates immediately set the tone for the match from the start with the more aggressive posture. He seemed eager to make the battle a slug-fest and undermine the quickness of the more experienced O'Brien. O'Brien was caught off-guard and took the worst of the milling for the first rounds. In the second round Bates sent O'Brien to the mat twice after hammer punches to O'Brien's jaw. Both times the

Philadelphia Jack O'Brien portrait, Wikimedia, ca. 1905

groggy O'Brien took the count before rising, quickly grabbing Bates in a clinch until the gong saved him from defeat. O'Brien stayed upright for the next three rounds while Bates carried the fight to him. In the sixth, Bates "sent a pile driving blow to the heart and

O'Brien fell to his knees gasping."[80] At the count of nine, O'Brien again saved himself by wrapping up Bates and holding until the timer's gong.

The clever and lighter O'Brien, however, regrouped, adapted and gave the best of it to Bates over the next four rounds, moving and darting his left jab in the face of Bates and escaping any further punishment from the heavier opponent. Some say Bates was too anxious and fought wildly from the seventh on, trying to put O'Brien away.

At fight's end one reporter felt the crowd anticipated a draw to be the call. Instead, referee Leroy Tozier slapped O'Brien on the back and loudly proclaimed him the winner. Almost simultaneous with the announcement, Bates rushed at Tozier and let go a right hook at the ref's head, which some say landed. With that the friends of both men scrambled into the ring "mixing merrily"[81] with fists flying in a free-for-all riot. The melee soon brought a rush of local police who made "judicious use of their clubs," indiscrimately knocking the heads of everyone in sight.[82]

News of the fight was on the sports page of papers across the country from California to Connecticut. It is unclear who requested a rematch although given the acrimonious outcome of their first bout, likely both Bates and O'Brien readily agreed. The second match would be 100 miles away from Dawson City in Fairbanks, Alaska, the home ground of Bates. Both men reportedly made the trip by horseback in time for the September 9th contest at the Fairbanks Club. But it was clear that expectations were high after the controversy of the first fight. One reporter wrote that "one of the largest crowds that has ever seen a sporting event in this locality was in attendance."[83]

Some papers dismissed Billy's challenge this second time calling Bates a "soft mark" for O'Brien who is "doomed for a beating."[84] Such news reports proved prophetic. O'Brien would not make the same mistake in underestimating the hard-hitting Bates a second time. Soon after the start of the first round, O'Brien's fast footwork and quick jabs rattled Billy. By the end of the fifth round, reports say Bates lost his temper and "wading in grabbed O'Brien around the waist and threw him violently to the floor of the ring," reminiscent of the Gotch/Slavin debacle. That stopped the match with Bates disqualified for his foul.[85] A "great exhibition" up to that point, satirized one reporter.[86]

O'Brien left the Klondike shortly after his victory, visited the Lewis and Clarke Exposition in Portland and then began touring California looking for possible matches. "Jack is always out after the money," declared the *Seattle Daily Times* but O'Brien's announced $13,000 windfall from his six months in the northern gold fields, he deemed as not up to his expectations.

While O'Brien was looking for some warmup matches in preparation for his shot at Bob Fitzsimmons, Billy Bates soon returned to San Francisco, hired to test the mettle of a heavyweight whose quick rise had been stunted following a sparring match with O'Brien in October 1905. Sam Spaulding was under the management of Biddy Bishop who promoted him as the next heavyweight world champion. But, after Spaulding was laid low in the practice meeting

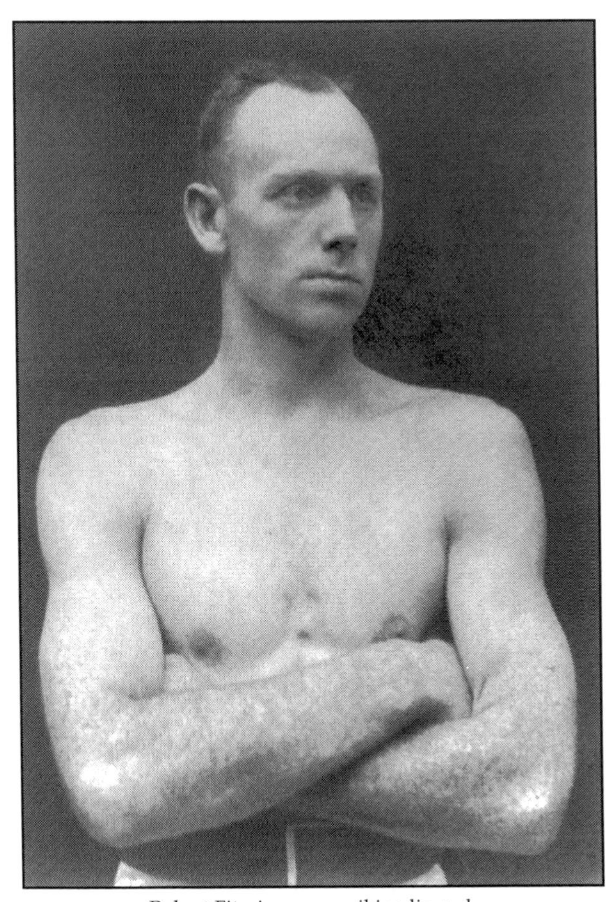

Robert Fitzsimmons, wikipedia, n.d.

with O'Brien, Biddy wanted to see how the "young giant" from the mines of Michigan matched with a seasoned veteran like Billy Bates before facing P.O. Davis in a sanctioned contest. Spaulding's massive frame stood six feet three inches tall and he weighed in at 237 pounds. By all accounts Spaulding took a good deal of punishment from Bates in the "red-hot milling" of the training sessions but withstood the wallops, giving back as good as he received.[87] That unfortunately did not stop Spaulding from kissing the canvas after a right hook to his jaw by Davis in the first round of their fight. Spaulding's championship aspirations, wrote one reporter, "went out in a burst of laughter."[88]

Even though he had a rough record coming out of the Yukon, Billy Bates' reputation was still solid among those who mattered. The *Seattle Daily Times* dubbed him the "Bruiser of the Yukon" and "light-heavyweight champion of Alaska" who "is considered the best fighter in the Yukon Territory and Alaska."[89]

It was now Bates' experience and not his wins which proved an asset. After Spaulding's loss, Bates became part of the training camp and corner men for Bob Fitzsimmons along with Young Croll and Harry Chester. Bates, in particular, counselled Fitzsimmons about O'Brien's style having some acquaintance with it. Nicknames for the British born Fitzsimmons, such as Ruby Robert, centered around his pale, freckled frame and balding sandy-colored hair. Fitzsimmons knocked out James Corbett in 1897 to gain the heavyweight title but lost it two years later to Jim Jeffries. He gained the light heavyweight crown beating George Gardner in 1903. *Ring Magazine* has ranked Fitzsimmons as number eight on the list of greatest punchers of all time.

O'Brien and Fitzsimmons were well matched in weight, with both around 165 pounds but Fitzsimmons was certainly the old man of the contest at the age of 42 versus the 27-year-old O'Brien. Billy Bates would turn 31 roughly two weeks before

Fitzsimmons and O'Brien met in the ring. The Fitzsimmons' camp worked at Croll's Gardens in Alameda, California. Upwards of 300 spectators crowded into the gym having paid fifty cents each to see "the old man," spar with Bates and boxer Harry Chester. Fitzsimmons was jaunty and confident of a victory wagering $5,000 on himself; confidence Billy Bates supported while speaking to the press on Bob's behalf. "Knowing what I do I think Fitzsimmons' punch is the thing that will bring home the money. He hasn't lost it, I assure you. I look for some dazzling work on O'Brien's part, but he will have to mix it if he expects to win, and, mark my words, Bob will nail him as he has nailed others before him."[90]

Mechanics' Pavilion in San Francisco was filled to capacity the night of December 20, 1905. Fitzsimmons seemed to have the best of it through the early rounds although knocked down in the eighth. Many in the crowd believed he was on his way to defending his title. Two severe blows, however, caught Fitzsimmons in the stomach and head in the 13th. The damage was not immediately apparent. Fitzsimmons walked to his corner and then collapsed, blood spilling from his mouth and nose. Bates and the other seconds "picked him up…looked at him and then stopped the fight….They laid Fitzsimmons on the floor a minute and then stood him on his feet." With the help of a "stimulant" Fitzsimmons recovered sufficiently to shake hands with O'Brien. O'Brien got the TKO decision and the light heavyweight title.[91] *Ring Magazine* elected O'Brien to its Hall of Fame in 1968 and ranked him as the number two all-time best light heavyweight. In 1909 O'Brien fought the legendary black champion Jack Johnson to a draw.

One boxing internet site shows Billy Bates finally beating Nick Burley in early January 1906 by a knockout and again in mid-August by TKO.[92]

Fitzsimmons reportedly put up the money for Bates to again battle O'Brien but there is no evidence that the fight happened. Although information on Bates' fistic contests becomes more scarce, he is listed as having fought other matches including one in early August 1906 in Fairbanks against a "wrestler of indifferent ability" named Chris Person who would be a "mutton dumpling" for Bates according to the *Seattle Daily Times* which still referred to Bates as a "comer." Bates finished off the wrestler in the second round.[93]

It's unclear how long Bates continued his boxing career but it appears that he began spending more time assisting in the mining operations of his brothers Sam and Gilley, known collectively as the Bates Bros. Company as his time in the ring was winding down.

The "Black Bear" of Iditarod

Nellie C. Bates and the Bates Brothers: Billy, Samuel and Gilbert

In August 1908, the Bates brothers tried their luck on Vault Creek roughly 15 miles north of Fairbanks but found it a bust financially. They determined to work for other operators until they could locate a better claim.[94] That more lucrative claim came two years later, away from the Yukon and back in Alaska territory at Otter Creek, situated between the small camps of Flat and Iditarod, Alaska. Iditarod is approximately 300 miles northwest of Anchorage. Between 1897 and 1907 more than 50 gold mining camps would spring up around Alaska with some like Nome and Fairbanks growing into major towns.[95] Charles Hawley wrote that "the pay on Otter Creek proved to be exceptionally wide, the widest paystreak ever mined in Alaska."[96]

John Beaton and Bill Dikeman made the find on Christmas day 1908 near the head of Otter Creek, a tributary of the Iditarod River along with alternate claims along the stream. The site was later dubbed Discovery. Word spread and by the summer of 1909 the new stampede brought prospectors who poured in to stake claims on Otter and its main tributaries. Between four and ten thousand men and women flooded into Flat by the spring of 1910 including the Bates brothers.[97] In April 1910, Billy Bates sent a

Flat City, Alaska, November 1912,
Alaska State Library, P-68-162, Basil C. Clemmons Photo Collection

telegram to brother Gilley from Otter Creek saying that he was "working night and day. Twenty five dollar pans common. Thin streak on bedrock."[98]

Lars Ostness arrived in the area as well and by spring 1910 had purchased No. 1 above Discovery on Otter Creek along with partners Jack Merritt, Angus McKenzie and the Bates Brothers, Gilley, Billy and Sam. One miner told a Skagway newspaper that the ground owned by the Bates boys was "about as good an anything he had seen in the country." One cleanup of their open cut (open pit) operation earned them 380 ounces of gold in 80 hours and 265 ounces in another 60 hours. The largest take was 1,300 ounces of gold worth $27,000. Lars was considered the best prospector of the bunch and would continue his relationship with the Bates brothers for several years.[99] A lawsuit by D. A. Campbell claiming ownership of half of the Otter Creek 1-A was resolved in that first summer of 1910, however the result was that in September of 1910 Merritt sold his one-third interest to Nellie Bates and the partnership between the Bates company, McKenzie and Merritt was dissolved. On September 18, 1910 the *Iditarod Pioneer* reported that the brothers had begun sluicing on the claim after an extended period of stripping. By that time, according to writer Terrie Hanke, Iditarod was a "well-appointed city" as was Flat. The boomtowns enjoyed "gaslights, telephones, newspapers, banks, restaurants, hotels, post office, pool hall and school."[100]

The Bates brothers and Nellie Bates continued to mine and lease properties along Otter Creek during this time including a transfer to Michael H. Marston in October 1910. Marston was an associate of Beaton in those early years at Otter Creek and subsequently the Bates brothers would form a partnership with Beaton as well even as they looked to expand their holdings to areas such as Black Creek near the community of Flat City. The partnership with Beaton was reportedly "very successful," largely due to the ability of foreman Ostnes.[101]

Gilley told an Anchorage newspaper in 1916 that he expected to retire after one more year. The newspaper ran a story on the "especially successful season" enjoyed by Gilley Bates and his brother Bill who were part of the "original stakers of Otter Creek." Thirty men worked for the company all season on the claim touted as "one of the best properties in the lower Iditarod country."[102] However, Gilley, and probably the Bates Bros. company, remained associated with John Beaton at Iditarod.

Gilley would assist Beaton after the worst maritime disaster on the west coast. Beaton's wife Florence and children, six-year-old Lauretta and four-year-old John Neil, boarded the steamer *Princess Sophia* which left Skagway, Alaska on October 23, 1918. Lars Ostnes was also planning on returning to Seattle on the ship but due to the pregnancy of his wife Elise, they decided to remain in Flat City. Shifting off course, the ship struck the Vanderbilt Reef at 2 a.m. on the 24th of October. Several vessels responded to their call for assistance but rough seas and an increasing storm prevented them from getting close enough to evacuate the *Sophia's* passengers. The ship began taking on water October 25th with its last SOS message at 5:20 that afternoon. The ship sank between 5:30 and 6 p.m. All 353 passengers on board were lost. Those bodies recovered were taken to Juneau where Gilley Bates identified the body of Florence Beaton but mistakenly ID'd Lauretta, an error corrected after John Beaton arrived. Her body was never recovered.[103]

It appears that since Nellie adopted the Bates name at this time, there was a probable common law relationship between her and Billy which began at Otter Creek since no marriage record has been found. Nellie would become notorious for a postal robbery in the 1920s but starting around 1910, she lived as the "wife" of Billy Bates and would for the next twelve years. Family postings identify Nellie Bates as Christina Wilhelmina Kruger. She was born on a farm outside Huntingburg, Indiana in April 1879. She acquired her first husband when she married

Otter Creek, between Discovery and Flat City, Alaska, September 1914, University. of Washington Special Collections, AWC4816

Henry L. Kaffenberger in April of 1900. It is believed that she left husband and home soon after for the adventures of the Klondike gold rush.[104] Her first occupation, and one she randomly practiced until the 1930s, was prostitution. Going by the name of Nellie C. Bates, she is shown on Polk city directories for Stanwood, Washington as being Billy's wife from 1914 until 1922 including the 1920 census. It seems clear that both Billy and Nellie traveled often to their holdings on Otter Creek, Alaska where Nellie is often listed as Mrs. William Bates. Billy's brothers were also found making the trek between Washington state and Alaska.[105]

Nellie Bates was a widely known figure throughout the towns and mining camps of the Klondike and Alaska. She and Billy Bates may have met earlier but they certainly came to know each other at Otter Creek and surrounding towns such as Flat City. Known,

Mining on Otter Creek near Iditarod, AK, between 1910 and 1930, University of Washington Special Collections, UW 41474

perhaps affectionately, as the "Black Bear" she had a reputation for her "dealings in prostitution, banking and mining claims;" an eclectic combination for a woman in the demanding and raw mining centers of the north. Editor Erin Turner wrote that Nellie was a "savvy businessperson" who had won a strong reputation in grub staking other miners at fair interest rates. "Men who knew her," said Turner, "liked her and respected her business acumen."[106]

Although Nellie C. Bates is still listed as the wife of Billy in a 1922 Polk city directory, by mid-summer of that year she is obviously back in Alaska, arriving in Juneau on the steamer *Queen* on July 17, 1922 in transit farther north. On July 26th the *Anchorage Daily Times* announced that Nellie had married Ernest Beattie, miner, hotelier and contracted supervisor of mail and gold shipments for the government and American Railway Express Company between the

Alaskan interior and the coast. Beattie vehemently denied any such wedding after returning to the area that August from a trip and the newspaper printed a retraction saying the dispatch they received from Seattle was a "rank canard."[107] It is unknown why or by whom the wedding announcement was sent but the last name of Beattie attached itself to Nellie and would be used interchangeably along with Bates thereafter.

Whatever her purpose, when mail carrier William Duffy, an employee of Ernie Beattie, arrived in Flat with his dog sled in late November 1922, Nellie saw a way out and asked if she and a friend could accompany Duffy on his trip. In the published account by Turner, it is surmised that Nellie Bates was seeking relief from the hard life she led as a prostitute—the "sporting life," was not a young woman's game and Nellie was approaching her mid-40s in 1922.[108] Perhaps, but this was a woman who seemed to always to be one step ahead in planning her next move or looking for the next opportunity. Escaping the hard life also doesn't take into account that she and Billy Bates recently dissolved whatever domestic arrangement they had followed for over a decade.

Mail carrier Duffy meant to rest himself and dogs before continuing on to McGrath which was roughly 84 miles from Flat to deliver a locked pouch to Thomas Atkins. Duffy agreed to let Nellie and the other prostitute accompany him on his sled. They wanted to reach Iditarod and find new prospects. Upon reaching McGrath, however, the postmaster did not have the right key for Atkins' mail bag and directed Duffy to return to Flat where the postmistress possessed the correct key for the locked pouch. Returning to Flat, the bag was opened and a surprised Duffy discovered its contents of $33,000, a fact the excited Duffy couldn't resist but divulge to Nellie. Continuing on Duffy and the women made Iditarod, parted with Nellie's companion and on December 30th stopped for the night 16 miles outside of town at a roadhouse owned by Bill Schermeyer.[109] By this time, the opportunistic Nellie surely must have considered how she might improve her own situation through Duffy's very seductive consignment. After helping to bed down the dogs alongside the sled in the barn, Schermeyer later told a trial jury that Nellie "walked into the home, motioned to [Schermeyer], and they went to the fish cache." "'I went in there,' [Schermeyer] testified, 'and she put her hand on my shoulder. Bill,' she asked me, 'are you game to make some money tonight? Nellie, I replied, I'm always game.'"

A few regulars gathered that evening at the roadhouse and after dinner settled in for a gambling card game of Pan while Nellie made them drinks. At around 9 p.m. as they got deeper into their cups, Nellie quietly snuck out to the barn where she relieved the pouch from the sled and hid it initially in the fish cache. Everyone left the next morning, including Duffy and Nellie on their way to McGrath. Schermeyer recovered the mail pouch, which he later destroyed, and buried the money. Nellie and Schermeyer later met in Flat and counted the cash.

Over the next eighteen months, the buried stash was recovered and re-buried in various locations including the roadhouse root cellar until early May of 1923. Difficult to find, Schermeyer mutilated some of the cash while exhuming it. He and Nellie had to dry the recovered bills and iron them after they became damp while interred. Placed now in fruit jars, the loot was this time buried in Schermeyer's garden, until late September of 1924.[110] Exhumed again and divvied up, some bills were then put in circulation to see if anybody, especially the authorities, noticed. Years later Flat resident Peter Bagoy remembered that during this time Schermeyer "appeared to be very prosperous, bestowing lavish gifts and grants of money to various people."[111] The pair felt confident that things had calmed about the robbery, however just before Schermeyer was set to leave for the States, Nellie told him that Duffy had grown suspicious and now accused them of taking the mail pouch and the money. He wanted a third of the cash to keep silent, a demand to which they both consented.[112]

Nellie Bates, Findagrave, n.d.
Posted by Steve Kruger.

Schermeyer then left the area, staying for a time in Oregon before moving on to San Diego and Mexico where illness and involvement with less than scrupulous women left him broke. Appeals for help to Nellie went unanswered. Stories of his movements, however, attracted the attention of postal inspectors who tracked him down in Los Angeles and arrested him. Duffy confessed to the crime and Nellie Bates' involvement. U.S. Marshal Lynn Smith was sympathetic and convinced Schermeyer to testify against Nellie.

The first trial of Nellie Bates took place in February 1927 in Fairbanks with Schermeyer as the chief witness for the prosecution. Ironically, mail supervisor Ernie Beattie, who had denied published rumors of marriage to Nellie, was both a witness for the prosecution and the defense. After nearly 50 hours of deliberation, the jury announced to the judge that they were hopelessly deadlocked. Attorneys later told the press that the jurors had voted 11 to 1 for conviction of Nellie Bates. While we do not know for sure how juror Mrs. Oscar Travel voted, it is interesting that she was the only woman on the panel.[113]

Prosecutors decided to re-try Nellie Bates. That trial took place again in Fairbanks in early 1928 and this time lasted 19 days. The jury found Nellie not guilty of being an accomplice to the postal theft in 1922 after deliberating for only three hours. The *Tacoma Daily Ledger* wrote that the trial "known as the 'Black Bear' case,... was one of the most costly in the annals of the Alaskan courts as the government brought witnesses by airplane."[114] It was several times more money than had been stolen according to editor Turner. She writes that after the first trial, Nellie Bates and William Duffy, the postal officer in charge of the pilfered dogsled, were living together in Flat and went to Fairbanks after hearing that new charges were about to be filed. Bates' attorney painted a picture of a defenseless woman pitted against the government, but Turner wrote that Nellie had many friends in Fairbanks and throughout the Alaskan interior who were reminded of the prostitute with the "heart of gold."[115]

William Duffy, Findagrave, n.d. Posted by Steve Kruger.

Nellie Bates and William Duffy are reported to have married in October 1929 and they are listed aboard the ship *President Van Buren* which sailed for Honolulu arriving on November 22, 1929—a possible honeymoon?[116] The married couple returned to the Iditarod district and continued mining in the area of Willow and Chicken Creeks. Nellie was no longer a prostitute as recollected by neighbors who knew them at that time. They were remembered as being quite well off financially. John Fullerton recalled that the couple "made a tour on the Graff Zeppelin, all the way to London, and to Egypt, all over the world. He couldn't get along without his Bull Durham tobacco, and she couldn't get along with her Hills Brothers Coffee." Duffy, said Fullerton, once bought the biggest Lincoln at a Seattle dealership, "peeling out cash from his pocket to pay for it." They spent their winters in Tucson, Arizona said Catherine Weimer. John Miscovich recalled that they loved horses and raised them at Santa Anita in California and it's believed that they moved to Arcadia, California in 1938.[117] William Duffy died in Los Angeles on September 8, 1940. Following her husband's death, Christina Wilhelmina Kruger-Kaffenberger-Bates-Beattie-Duffy returned to her Huntingburg, Indiana hometown where she buried her husband and is said to have built a brick home. She returned to California where she died in San Diego on April 20, 1867. After her funeral, her body was cremated with her ashes returned to Huntingburg and buried beside Duffy. She was 88 years old.[118]

Bill Schermeyer, who turned state's evidence was the only one to serve time for the theft of the money and entered McNeil Island Federal Penitentiary on April 14, 1928 and was released a year later.[119] He is reported to have died shortly afterwards. There doesn't appear to be any evidence of a trial and it is likely that Shermeyer had a plea agreement with prosecutors for his testimony.

The Black Bear of the Iditarod was a true sourdough mused editor Turner. Several of her interviewed neighbors acknowledged that she was involved in the theft of the mail pouch but for some it was an example of David again beating the Goliath of the American governmental giant. Certainly it is a lesson that just sometimes, crime does succeed—timing being everything,

As for Billy Bates, whose last name had been bantered across newspaper headlines for a couple of years, he doesn't appear to have mourned the loss of Nellie for long. Whether their parting was mutual or just based on Nellie's own frustration and wanderlust, a year after her departure as his "wife," Bill Bates married Lillian H. Deiner, a hair dresser in King County, Washington in June 1923. Bill and Lillian owned a dairy farm north of Stanwood by 1925 with brother Sam's farm just across from them along Pacific Highway. Bill and Lillian, however, were splitting their time between Stanwood and the Shelton area in Mason County.

The 1930 census shows Bill, Lillian and brother Gilley living in Northside, Washington in Mason County where Bill and Gilley give their occupations as loggers. They may have been assisting older brother Alex who stayed in the logging business most of his life and died in nearby Shelton in 1935. Gilbert married his second wife Levine Munson in adjacent Pierce County in early January of 1930. The Munson farm was situated just north of the Bates brothers' property in Stanwood. Gilley's first wife Emma Holmstead died in 1920.[120] Gilley Bates worked his farm near Stanwood until 1942 when he moved into the town. He was 80 when he died in Mt. Vernon on June 20, 1951.

Sam married Mercedes Rogers at Otter Creek on September 15, 1911. Mercedes was one-quarter Snoqualmie. Her father Lee Rogers ran the Forks Hotel on the south fork of the Stillaguamish River in what was then Haller City near Arlington. Sam died of a lung abscess on December 20, 1951 in Everett where he was hospitalized for tuberculous. He was 75 years old. Mercedes died in Stanwood on April 3, 1965. It must have been a cool but pleasant day on October 12, 1944 since Billy decided to do some work

Georgia and Mercedes Rogers, n.d.
Ancestry.com

in his garden. The former champion of the Yukon didn't finish however, dying of a heart attack at 4 p.m. that afternoon at the age of 69.[121]

There were no lengthy eulogies for the brothers; their obituaries are cleanly factual but lacking any recitations of their value to the community or personal attributes. Still, they had worked shoulder to shoulder, and sometimes glove to face, with iconic figures in the pioneer worlds of mining and sports. The spotlight of history did not fall on them but they were standing close to the light. Their stories, like so many, show the perseverance and effort that went into just living in this time period. Lives perhaps deemed average in one era, can amaze and awe us today; re-told they are restored and revived--and they are remembered.

Conclusion

For some of the men from Stanwood and the surrounding area, the stampede to the northern gold fields was a moment of adventure and danger and the profound hope for what tomorrow could deliver. Of the estimated 100,000 gold seekers who risked the hardships of the Yukon, the men of Stanwood would be only a statistical anecdote. A very few found the wealth they imagined but they brought back their experiences and what resources they accumulated to their homes and enhanced their community. Does this mean that Stanwood's progress of the early 20th century was due totally to the wealth which returned with the stampeders? No, of course not. But their participation, money and energy which they did infuse into the economy of the area certainly was a contributing factor to the boom of the town and its progress and prosperity during this time.

Stanwood had been disappointed when the Seattle & Montana Railroad (later Great Northern) skirted coming to the town and instead laid track and established a depot a mile east of Stanwood's main center. Nearby Arlington did initially gain more advantage when another rail line enabled it to grab much of the upriver trade that had been Stanwood's in previous years.[122] An 1892 fire devastated Stanwood's downtown, impeding its progress as well. Stanwood citizens regrouped and adapted nicely, however. As the Yukon gold rush ushered Seattle from its financial doldrums, brought on by the 1893 Panic, small western Washington towns would also

Photo by Juleen, Bank of Stanwood on the right, H&H tracks in foreground
Stanwood Area Historical Society #92.41.160, ca. 1920

use the proceeds of hometown gold seekers to lift them up economically. As mentioned, in 1904 Henry Anderson and others established the First Bank of Stanwood in a new brick building. The bank was a major investor in the town's H & H Railroad which was either the shortest steam rail line in the state (and perhaps the world) or the best street car system for a town its size as designated by some news accounts. Regardless, it provided the link between the growing mills along the Stillaguamish River and the rail depot to its east.[123]

The rich, black, soil around Stanwood, however, did attract most of the attention by promotional articles concerning the area. The soil's fertility was a result of thousands of years of accumulated river silt in this delta region. Many of the hopeful Klondikers did invest in this mainstay of American wealth—land;

its acquisition and development nearly ubiquitous among those who returned from the north. A Tacoma reporter exited the train in Stanwood in 1905 and wrote of the fields being alive with men and teams, harrowing, sowing and planting. From oats to hay to dairy operations the promises of the farms seemed endless.[124] This era of agriculture followed the initial wave of loggers which first populated the region and that industry would continue for several years.

The additional assets from their mining adventures permitted these ranchers to expand operations. They also created businesses or invested in the efforts of others. Local Stanwood historian Alice Essex wrote that at the advent of 1903, "new social and community clubs were appearing, more buildings were dotting the horizon and, most important of all, enthusiasm and prosperity reigned."[125] Stanwood benefited from the wealth, marginal or great, brought back by the Klondike seekers. The gold they sought helped spawn a golden age for Stanwood in the early years of the 20th century.

In July 1907, *the Seattle Daily Times* wrote that "there is probably no town in the Northwest of its size that has made greater progress or a more healthy and rapid growth in the past two years than Stanwood."[126] There were two banks by that time, the Bank of Stanwood, with Henry Anderson as its president and the First Scandia Bank. The former had improved its assets from $16,523 in 1904 when it was founded to nearly $165,000 three years later.[127] By 1907 there were four general stores, three large hardware stores, an up-to-date hospital under the guidance of surgeon Dr. O.R. Allen, two livery stables, three lodge halls, several secret societies, two lumber mills with nine

The Bon Ton saloon, E. Tolin Proprietor, Stanwood, WA, 1900,
Photograph by John Wagness, Stanwood Area Historical Society #92.40A.08

other lumber and shingle mills in surrounding areas. The town was well lit by electricity with thousands of dollars allocated for expanded streets, sidewalks and crosswalks. The town also boasted three other hotels, six restaurants and five saloons. The towering five-story Palace Hotel dominated the view near the river's wharf. Stanwood's shipyard, which employed 25 workers, built the steamer *Gleaner* in 1907 and the *Harvester* five years later in 1912.[128] The roughly 1200 citizens of the town in that same year had no bond indebtedness and were able to install a new sewage system for $6,000 and to begin permanently improving their streets paving with "Warrenite" at a cost of $9,000.[129]

Palace Hotel, Stanwood, WA, 1900, Photograph by John Wagness,
Stanwood Area Historical Society #92.40.10

One historical event does not account for all the change that comes to a community. There are obviously myriad factors but it is hard to underestimate the value to Stanwood and its growth and prosperity which was invigorated by the Stanwood stampeders. To understand local history is to understand the personal effect on those who lived it in their respective eras; the choices they made and the consequences of those choices. History is not just a litany of events and dates but the underlying decisions of people and how that effected their lives, their communities and the larger society for good or for ill.

Endnotes

[1] Thomas Hart Benton as quoted by John Waters, "Stampede: Gold Fever and disaster in the Klondike," August 07, 2021, Stampede: Gold Fever and Disaster in the Klondike | RealClearDefense.
[2] T.E. Lawrence, Seven Pillars of Wisdom (Hertfordshire, England: Wordsworth Editions, LTD., 1935), p. 7.
[3] *Seattle Post-Intelligencer*, July 17, 1897.
[4] Pierre Berton, *The Klondike Fever: The Life and Death of the Last Great Gold Rush*, Pickle Partners Publishing, 2015, pp. 109-113. Howard Blum explains that the term Klondike is a corruption of the Hän tribe's term for the river. They called it Throndiuk (or Tr'ondëk) meaning "Hammer Water" or hammerstone water in recognition of the fence of stakes Natives would hammer across the shallow waters to hold their gill nets. Trappers and prospectors could not pronounce the guttural Indian term and mangled it coming out as Klonkike. See Howard Blum, *The Floor of Heaven: A True Tale of the Last Frontier and the Yukon Gold Rush*, (New York: Broadway Paperbacks, 2011), p. 257.
[5] *Seattle Post-Intelligencer*, July 17, 1897.
[6] *Seattle Daily Times*, July 18, 1897. The *Post-Intelligencer* reported that Henry had sold a half interest in #32 for $43,000 which he also carried to Seattle. It is the thought of this writer that Norwegian Henry Christian Anderson was sometimes confused with Swede Carl Johan Anderson (1859-1937) dubbed the "Lucky Swede" by his cohorts in the Klondike. This may have been the case of the *Post-Intelligencer* whose reporter found a Henry Anderson onboard the Portland but identified him as a "native of Sweden" who had sold a half-interest of his Eldorado Creek claim and was returning to Seattle. The Lucky Swede was also known as Charlie Anderson as was H. C. Anderson who lived and worked in Seattle and Stanwood, Washington. Carl (Charlie) Anderson was duped while drunk in purchasing a claim along Eldorado Creek thought by its owners as a bust. That claim, #29, turned out to possess a very rich vein of gold producing an estimated 1.5 million dollars. Writer Hans Högman wrote that what the Swede "didn't lose in his marriage to one of the town prostitutes, Grace Drummond, he lost in the great

San Francisco earthquake of April 15, 1906." See Högman, The Emigration from Sweden to the USA, Swedish History - Hans Högman (hhogman.se).

[7] Obituary of Henry C. Anderson, *Stanwood Tidings*, August 21, 1914;. *History of Snohomish County*, vol. II, William Whitfield (ed.) (Chicago, Seattle: Pioneer Publishing Company, 1926), 631. The predominance of information concerning Henry Anderson does not reveal what his middle initial C stood for. Regardless, and ironically, he was given the moniker of "Klondike Charley" by Stanwood residents after his success in the Yukon. There are, however, two documents signed by Henry that present his full name: his form for naturalization on April 12, 1912 and the marriage certificate for his daughter Agnes on December 23, 1933. On both of these official documents, he signs his full name as Henry Christian Anderson.

[8] A. J. Roan, Before the Klondike there was Forty Mile, *North of 60 Mining News*, accessed August 20, 2021, Before the Klondike there was Forty Mile - North of 60 Mining News (miningnewsnorth.com); *Seattle Daily Intelligencer*, June 12, 1895.

[9] Gold Placers of the Historical Fortymile River Region, Alaska—1996, U. S. Geological Survey Bulletin 2125, pp. 9-10.

[10] Berton, *The Klondike Fever*, p. 75.

[11] *Seattle Daily Times*, July 20, 1898; obituary of J. P. Anderson, *Twin City News*, November 24, 1938; *Seattle Daily Intelligencer*, July 17, 1897.

[12] *Daily Morning Alaskan*, August 15, 1901; W. A. Waiser, "Dredgery": Researching the Life and Times of Canadian Number Four, *Archivaria*, Journal of the Association of Canadian Archivists, #22, (Summer, 1986), "Dredgery": Researching the Life and Times of Canadian Number Four | Archivaria, accessed, August 22, 2021.

[13] Pete MacKenzie interview with Grace Cornwell, *Stanwood Camano News*, March 30, 1983.

[14] Whitfield, *History of Snohomish County*, vol. II, 607.

[15] *Seattle Daily Times*, July 20, 1898.

[16] *Seattle Daily Intelligencer*, August 13, 1899; There is a H. C. Anderson traveling on the Admiral Sampson from Seattle, see *Alaska Daily Empire*, February 26, 1914.

[17] *Seattle Daily Times*, May 2, 1900; Alice Essex, *The Stanwood Story*, vol. I, pg. 25; *Seattle Daily Times*, December 21, 1912. The

paper wrote that July 1, 1899 was when the first rail train reached Lake Bennett.

[18] Obituary files of the Stanwood Area Historical Society; *Washington Standard* (Olympia, WA), April 4, 1913.

[19] Obituary for Ida Anderson, *Stanwood Tidings*, March 20, 1913, files of the Stanwood Area Historical Society; Dennis Conroy, "Henry C. 'Klondike' Anderson," Echoes #16, (fall 1999), Stanwood Area Historical Society files.

[20] *Seattle Daily Times*, March 24, 26, 27, 1913.

[21] *Washington Standard* (Olympia, Washington), April 4, 1913; Katherine Beck, "Hazzard, Linda Barfield (1867-1938), Historylink.org, Essay 7955, posted October 26, 2006, retrieved September 3, 2021.

[22] Conroy, "Henry C. 'Klondike' Anderson," Echoes #16; Peggy Wendel, *Everett Herald*, June 24, 1999; *Chicago Sun*, August 10, 1945, Florida death certificate accessed via Ancestry.com. Agnes was cremated and her ashes taken to Chicago. The mission of the Annie Wright School, which opened in 1884, was to "make possible Christian education for the rising generation of daughters of the pioneers." At a Brokaw family gathering in Tacoma in 1924 Mamie Brokaw, widow of W. C. Brokaw who died in 1920, is listed as the ward of Agnes Anderson. See *Tacoma Daily Ledger*, August 24, 1924.

[23] *Klondike Nugget* Anniversary Issue, November 1, 1899; *History of Snohomish County*, vol. II, pp. 658-659. Bernard Estby, who often went by the name Ben, was born in February 1868 in Ottertail, Minnesota although in one census he gives his birthdate as May 1867. His father Anders moved the family to Washington around 1886 moving to Norman roughly two years later. Bernard is listed as living in the Yukon territories in a 1901 Canadian census. He is an engineer who reports having arrived in Canada in 1898. In 1910 he is living with John Lee and his family in Fairbanks, Alaska. By that time he is known as a pioneer driller becoming sole owner of the Craig-Crook-Estby Keystone drill in 1913. He owned a patent filed in 1905 for an improvement of the rotary engine. In 1912 he made an unsuccessful bid for state political office. He ran as a Socialist although his father was a life-long Republican. See the 1901 Canadian census and 1910 Federal Census, Ancestry.com; *Fairbanks Daily Times*, February 20 and May 10, 1913; US779400A - Rotary engine - Google Patents.

[24] Ibid; Whitfield's history states that Lee's daughter Olive H. was born in Everett on May 1, 1906. However, the will of John Lee, dated April 30, 1926, says that she was his adopted daughter. See John Lee, Wills and Probates records, 1851-1970, Ancestry.com.
[25] Jon Hahn, interview with Ken and Pat Wagness, *Seattle Post-Intelligencer*, October 6, 1990, July 18, 1997; Obituary of John Lee, files of the Stanwood Area Historical Society archives.
[26] Photographers of Fargo, N.D., Institute for Regional Studies, North Dakota State University, Fargo, 2001. Accessed September 4, 2021. Untitled Document (ndsu.edu).
[27] *Tacoma Daily Ledger*, June 2, 1887, November 8, 1887; *Tacoma News Tribune*, February 24, 1890, March 12, 1890. A city directory for Seattle shows Berge Lee and family living in Seattle in 1887; Polk city directories for Seattle / Tacoma, 1889-1897.
[28] *Tacoma Daily Ledger*, November 22, 1891; *Tacoma Daily News*, January 2, 1891. Polk city directories for Seattle / Tacoma, 1889 – 1897.
[29] Jon Hahn, interview with Ken and Pat Wagness, *Seattle Post-Intelligencer*, July 18, 1997; Chilkoot Pass: The "Golden Staircase," University of Washington, Chilkoot Pass: The "Golden Staircase" — UW Libraries (washington.edu); Ross Anderson, *Seattle Times*, July 7, 1997.
[30] Thomas Ostenson Stine, *Scandinavians on the Pacific, Puget Sound*, (Seattle, Washington: 1900), p. 146.
[31] Agnes Deans Cameron, *The New North: Being Some Account of a Woman's Journey through Canada to the Arctic*, 1909, reprinted in 2018, p. 43, digitized by Project Gutenberg, 2004, The Project Gutenberg eBook of The New North, by Agnes Deans Cameron.
[32] Whitfield, *History of Snohomish County*, vol. II, pp. 189, 715; Obituary files of the Stanwood Area Historical Society.
[33] *Seattle Post-Intelligencer*, March 7, 1898; *Seattle Daily Times*, January 23, 1898. In 1893, Willis Thorp installed "a water wheel variety of electric generator" at Gold Creek near Juneau to supply electricity to area residents and merchants. A year later in 1894 Thorp was a founder of the Alaska Electric Light and Power Company.
[34] *Seattle Post-Intelligencer*, March 6 and 7, 1898. See *Alaska Journal of Commerce* (August 2007), "Hydro Power in Southeast Intrigues Leaders," August 25, 2007, available digitally at Alaska Journal |

Hydro power in Southeast intrigues leaders
[35] Ancestry.com; Polk City Directories for Seattle, 1897; *Seattle Daily Intelligencer*, September 6, 1896.
[36] Polk city directories: *Pacific Motor Boat* magazine, v. 8, No. 4 (January 1916) page 21; *Seattle Daily Times*, November 10, 1920. James Esary and his brothers Tom, Daniel and Andrew had logging operations around Lake Union, Green Lake, Camano Island and Vancouver Island. By the years of 1904 and 1905 James was manager of the Camano Commercial Company and the Camano Land and Lumber Company. In November 1900 their mill in La Conner was destoroyed by fire. In 1907 fires swept Camano threatening to sweep every stick of timber from the island. The Esarys lost three-fourths of their railroad and two million feet of cedar at a value of $50,000. A year later, James Esary sold the Camano Land and Lumber Company to Frank Van Cleve and Sons. His association with master mariner Howard B. Lovejoy of Coupeville, began approximatly in 1906 and the creation of the Island Transportation Company. By 1918, a year before Lovejoy's death, James Esary was also Vice President of the Ballard Shipbuilding Company and Lovejoy was the General Manager. See: Margaret Riddle, History link.org, Essay 9587; Polk city directories listing Esary, 1905 - 1907, Ancestry.com; *Seattle Post-intelligencer,* December 17, 1900; *Morning Olympian,* Agust 8, 1907; *Seattle Daily Times* June 16,1918; *The Lumber World* magazine, vol. 6, No. 1 (April 15, 1908) page 14, The Lumber World - Google Books.
[37] Addresses of Francis Giard, Jr. to members of the Stanwood Area Historical Society, fall 1994, Oral history files of the SAHS; Whitfield, History of Snohomish County, vol. II, p. 658; *Seattle Daily Times,* March 16, 1901; "Town of Chinik, now known as Golovin," historical notes, University of Washington, digital collections, Town of Chinik, now known as Golovin - Alaska, Western Canada and United States - University of Washington Digital Collections. The families of the Giards and Liens were related and migrated from the Midwest (Minnesota and later Dakota territory), arriving at Stanwood in 1889. They had gone north and taken the Canadian railway system across Canada to the west coast. The sister of Nils Lien (1837 – 1918) Elen Anna Bruun Mathiasdatter, married Francis Giard Sr., father of the subject and Klondiker of this section.

[38] J. Kingston Pierce, "Panic of 1893, Seattle's First Great Depression," Essay 2030, Historylink.org, November 24, 1999, Panic of 1893: Seattle's First Great Depression - HistoryLink.org. Archie Binns from his book *Northwest Gateway*, quoted by Pierce in *Columbia, The Magazine of Northwest History*, (Winter 1993-94): Vol. 7, No. 42. Panic of 1893.pdf.

[39] David M. Buerge, Peter Henning, Jr. (ed.), *The Builder: The Life of Peter Henning, 1868-1955, pp. 9-18.* No copyright date is listed and the book appears to be privately printed by the family. Buerge had access to personal family history especially "Autobiography of the First Twenty Years of the Life of Peter Henning, 1868-1888" which was dictated by Peter Henning to his wife Nannie around the year 1950. Nordstorm tried his own hand at mining claims in the Yukon only to have his claim challenged. Selling out he returned to Seattle and with his profits began his shoe store with partner Carl Wallin in 1901.

[40] Buerge, *The Builder*, pp. 20-22; National Park Service, "Series: Chilkoot Tramways," Series: Chilkoot Tramways (nps.gov), accessed September 22, 2021.

[41] Buerge, *The Builder*, 21-28; Obituary of Peter Henning, *Everett Herald*, March 22, 1955.

[42] Buerge, *The Builder*, 29; *Daily Alaskan*, October 22, 1908.

[43] Buerge, *The Builder*, 30; Henning obituary, *Everett Herald*, March 22, 1955.

[44] Buerge, *The Builder*, 35-60; Henning obituary, *Everett Herald*, March 22, 1955; Polk city directories, 1937, 1941, 1950.

[45] *An Illustrated History of Skagit and Snohomish Counties, THEIR PEOPLE, THEIR COMMERCE AND THEIR RESOURCES* (Interstate Publishing Company, 1906), pp. 979-980.

[46] *Douglas Island News*, September 13, 1899; January 18, 1899.

[47] *An Illustrated History of Skagit and Snohomish Counties*, 979; *Douglas Island News*, September 13, 1899; *Seattle Daily Intelligencer*, December 6, 1899.

[48] Essex, *The Stanwood Story*, vol. 1, p. 74; *An Illustrated History of Skagit and Snohomish Counties*, 980.

[49] Jan Olof G. Lindström and Karen L. Olson, *The Platinum King: Andrew Olson's Story*, (Bothell, WA: Book Publishers Network, 2004), pp. 75-135; Charles Hawley and Karen Olson, "Anders Olof Olsson: Andrew Olson, (1885-1981)," 2005, Andrew Olson (alaskamininghalloffame.org).

[50] Sarah Hurst, *North of 60 Mining News*, January 30, 2005, 'The Platinum King: Andrew Olson's Story' - North of 60 Mining News (miningnewsnorth.com).
[51] Lindstrom and Olson, *The Platinum King*, 224-232, 240-241, 257.
[52] Ibid., 250-256, 297.
[53] Lindstrom and Olson, *The Platinum King*, 298-300; Hurst, *North of 60 Mining News.*
[54] Whitfield, *History of Snohomish County,* vol. II, 223-224; Mrs. Neil A. MacLeod, *The Glengarry News*, October 13, 1933; See also: J. H. Macdonnell, *Sketches Illustrating the Early Settlement and History of Glengarry in Canada,* (Montreal: W. Foster Brown & Co., 1893).
[55] Whitfield, *History of Snohomish County,* vol. II, 223-224; Polk city directories for Stanwood 1907-1915; Vivian Berg, "Beginnings of Catholic church here traced," n.d., files of the Stanwood Area Historical Society.
[56] *San Francisco Examiner*, May 19, 1903.
[57] *Stanwood Tidings*, November 13, 1914.
[58] *Daily Alaska Dispatch* [Juneau], October 26, 1905; *San Francisco Chronicle*, November 16, 1905; *Seattle Daily Times,* October 26, 1906.
[59] *San Francisco Call Bulletin*, February 17, 1903.
[60] *Klondike Nuggett*, July 1, 1901; Michael Gates, *Yukon News*, Frank 'Paddy' Slavin: The 'Sydney Cornstalk,' July 27, 2017, Frank 'Paddy' Slavin: The 'Sydney Cornstalk' – Yukon News (yukon-news.com).
[61] *Klondike Nuggett*, September 7, 1901.
[62] Mike Chapman on Frank Gotch – YouTube, retrieved June 5, 2021.
[63] Charles "Tiv" Kreling, *San Francisco Examiner*, December 19, 20, 21, 22, 25, 1917. Kreling knew the wrestling game, having been a wrestler himself and a trainer at the Olympic Auditorium in San Francisco. He was also a coach for boxers Jimmy Britt and Owen Moran. His published photographs of the Yukon brought him notoriety. See, Tiv Kreling, Findagrave.
[64] *Twin City News*, July 26, 1951. Joe Carroll Marsh wrote to Sam Bates following the death of Gilley Bates in 1951 saying that he had never forgotten spending time in the Bates' home and the "wonderful meals" served by mother Bates. Sam Bates described Marsh as a man of "great physical and mental prowess"

who held several college degrees. Marsh was close to all three brothers during their time in Dawson City and had maintained those ties over the years. Marsh also listed Arthur Buel (1877-1952) as a good friend of Billy Bates. Buel was a noted editorial cartoonist who got his start in the Yukon while in his early 20s before working for newspapers in Nevada in 1905 and back to California in 1908. He was a boxer himself and enjoyed engaging in amateur bouts in mining camps. See: Arthur V. Buel - Biography of a Nevada Caricaturist | ONE (onlinenevada.org)

[65] Mark Hewitt, et al, Gotch in the Klondike, wrestlingclassics.com; *Baltimore Sun*, March 29, 1902. Joe Carroll Marsh was indicted in 1909 as part of the infamous Mabray Gang known for fixing sports events from boxing to horse races. Marsh spent 18 months in jail after pleading guilty in March 1910 to postal fraud. See Hewitt and Jimmy Wheeler, Biography: 0004 - Published: July 2014 - #PWHS (prowrestlinghistoricalsociety.com).

[66] *San Francisco Call Bulletin*, February 17, 1903; *San Francisco Chronicle*, February 26, 1903.

[67] *The Register*, (Adelaide, South Australia) March 29, 1902 accessed on Chapter XIII. (slavens.net); *The Yukon World* (Dawson City, Y.T.), March 24, 1907 accessed on Journal of Combative Sport: Gotch in Talk of Dawson (ejmas.com); *Sacramento Bee*, February 2, 1917.

[68] *Daily Alaska Dispatch*, June 12, 1902. *The Klondike Nugget* on May 9, 1902 praised Bates' earlier efforts prior to being tarnished by the Burley fiasco. It reported that "Bates is by no means a stranger in Dawson, he having resided here for the past two or three years. He has gone up against such men as Billy Perkins and Frank Slavin, his go with the latter being a ten-round draw and of one of the [indecipherable] battles ever seen in the city. He has the advantage of youth, good wind, a long reach, has never abused the magnificent physique with which Nature has endorsed him, and never could be called a quitter."

[69] *San Francisco Chronicle*, February 14, 1903.

[70] *San Francisco Chronicle*, January 28, 1903, February 14, 1903, February 26, 1903; *San Francisco Call Bulletin*, February 15, 1903, February 17, 1903. This "Perkins" was Will or Billy Perkins whom Slavin severely beat on July 3, 1900 and died 18 months later from his injuries.

[71] *Oregon Journal*, March 3, 1903; *Oregon Journal*, March 10, 1903.

[72] *Seattle Daily Times*, August 2, 1903.
[73] *Daily Morning Alaskan* [Skagway], September 29, 1903.
[74] *Daily Morning Alaskan*, October 9, 1903.
[75] *Seattle Daily Times*, October 11, 1904, October 17, 1904, May 15, 1902, August 24, 1902.
[76] *Seattle Daily Times*, October 17, 1904.
[77] *Seattle Daily Times*, October 21, 1904.
[78] *Yukon World* cited by *Daily Alaska Dispatch*, August 4, 1905.
[79] *Daily Alaska Dispatch*, August 15, 1905.
[80] *Seattle Daily Times*, August 30, 1905.
[81] Ibid.
[82] *Waterbury* [CT] *Evening Democrat*, September 2, 1905.
[83] *Baltimore Sun*, September 13, 1905.
[84] *Duluth New-Tribune*, September 3, 1905.
[85] *Topeka State Journal*, September 15, 1905.
[86] *Baltimore Sun*, September 13, 1905.
[87] *San Francisco Chronicle*, November 16, 1905; *Evening News* (San Jose, CA), November 16, 1905; *Spokane Chronicle*, October 13, 1905.
[88] *Spokane Herald*, October 13, 1905; *Salt Lake Herald*, December 3, 1905.
[89] *Seattle Daily Times*, October 1, 1905.
[90] *Baltimore American*, December 17, 1905.
[91] *Columbus* [Ohio] *Dispatch*, December 21, 2021.
[92] Boxrec.com, BoxRec: Nick Burley. Burley's real name was Nicholas Barovich. He died March 7, 1911 at the age of 35 of a heart attack and was buried in the Duwamish Poor Farm Cemetery of King County, WA.
[93] *Seattle Daily Times*, August 26, 1906; *Fairbanks Daily Times*, August 4, 1911 in flashback to 1906.
[94] *Fairbanks Daily Times*, August 12, 1908.
[95] Meeting of Frontiers: Alaska – Gold Rush (loc.gov).
[96] Charles Hawley, John Beaton, 1875 – 1945, Alaska Mining Hall of Fame, first published in the *The Alaska Miner*, (December 2001), Alaska Mining Hall of Fame Inductees - John Beaton.
[97] Ibid.
[98] *Fairbanks Daily News-Miner*, April 16, 1959. A look back 49 years ago on that date.
[99] *Daily Alaskan*, May 12, 1910; Lars Ostnes (1883-1972), Curtis J. Freeman, Jeane Ostnes Rinear and Eleanor Ostnes Vistaunet,

Lars Ostnes (alaskamininghalloffame.org). On May 14, 1910. The *Daily Alaskan* reported that pans on the Bates property were running as high as $80 a pan.

[100] *Iditarod Pioneer*, September 4, 18 and October 9, 1910. Terrie Hanke, "Eye on the Trail: Iditarod and Flat @ Mile 432," Eye on the Trail: Iditarod and Flat @ Mile 432 – Iditarod.

[101] *Iditarod Pioneer*, October 9, 1910; Hawley, John Beaton.

[102] *Anchorage Daily Times*, October 21, 1916.

[103] Hawley, John Beaton; *Juneau Empire*, October 10, 2018.

[104] The *Herald* (Jasper, Indiana), August 26, 1967.

[105] *Iditarod Pioneer*, January 22, 1911, Wm. Bates and wife arrive at hotel in Iditarod; *Daily Alaskan*, October 14, 1915. Mr. and Mrs. Wm. Bates in Skagway on their way outside for the winter. Oddly, the paper also notes a daughter traveling with them; *Seward Gateway*, January 29, 1916, Nellie Bates among the passengers on the *S.S. Alameda*; *Iditarod Pioneer*, March 11, 1916, Mrs. Nellie Bates on list of letters waiting for pickup at the Flat post office; *Anchorage Daily Times*, February 12, 1920, Nellie Bates registered at Hotel Anchorage having come from Seattle. With her varied names, confusion often surrounds the elusive Nellie. At least one Ancestry.com site does show William Bates as one of her husbands along with Henry Kaffenberger who she married in Posey County, Indiana in April 1900. Findagrave gives Christina Wilhelmina Kruger's birthdate as April 10, 1879 in Huntingburg, Indiana daughter of George Frederick Kruger and Wilhelmina Ahrens Kruger, although she will offer different birth years in various records. She preferred to go by the name of Nellie. See Steve Kruger, Findagrave. This writer was able to confirm that the same woman known as "Black Bear,"who will marry William Forsyte Duffy in October 1929 is the same woman who lived as the common law wife of Billy Bates. In the 1920 federal census, while Bates' wife, she gives her name as Nellie C. Bates, born 1880 in Indiana. Her father's birthplace is given as "at sea." In the 1930 federal census as the wife of William Duffy, she gives her name as Christine Nellie born 1882 in Indiana. Her father's birthplace is given as "atlantic ocean." An extremely rare coincidence or she's the same woman.

[106] Black Sheep of Alaska, alaskaweb.org/blacksheep/index.html; "Nellie 'Black Bear' Bates and William Schermeyer," *Outlaw Tales of the Old West: Fifty True Stories of Desperadoes,*

Crooks, Criminals, and Bandits, Erin Turner (ed.), *(Helena, Montana: TWODOT Books, 2016), p. 14.*

[107] *Alaska Daily Empire* [Juneau], July 17 and 18, 1922; *Anchorage Daily Times*, July 26, 1922, August 8, 1922; *Seattle Daily Times*, January 2, 1927.

[108] *Outlaw Tales of the Old West, p. 14.*

[109] Ibid, 15-16.

[110] Bill Schermeyer testiimony, *Kusko Times* (Takotna, AK), (taken from the *Fairbanks News-Miner)*, March 5, 1927. A fish cache is a small structure or shed raised off the ground usually on stilts, used for storage of food and equipment meant to protect against bears and other animals. The game Pan, also called Panguingue, is a variation of rummy games, only played in western states.

[111] Schermeyer testimony, *Kusko Times*, March 5, 1927, 17-18; Peter Bagoy, interview by Rolfe G. Buzzell, August 28, 1993, Flat and Iditarod Oral History Interviews, 1993-1995, BLM-Alaska Open File Report 66, Library_Alaska_OpenFileReport66.pdf (blm.gov).

[112] Schermeyer testimony, *Kusko Times*, March 5, 1927.

[113] *Kusko Times*, February 12, 1927.

[114] *Tacoma Daily Ledger* and *Seattle Daily Times*, March 20, 1928.

[115] *Outlaw Tales of the Old West, 20-21.*

[116] Arriving and Departing Passenger Lists, 1900-1959 available via Ancestry.com

[117] John Fullerton, interview, July 27, 1993, Catherine Weimer interview January 18, 1994 and John Miscovich, interview July 26, 1993 by Rolfe Buzzell, Flat and Iditarod Oral History Interviews, 1993-1995, BLM-Alaska Open File Report 66, (April 1997), Library_Alaska_OpenFileReport66.pdf (blm.gov); The *Herald* (Jasper, IN), August 26, 1967.

[118] Kruger, Findagrave; The *Herald* (Jasper, Indiana), August 26, 1967; Evansville (Indiana) Press, September 11, 1940. William Forsyth Duffy was born in Forsyth, Montana on August 26, 1882. According to the *Monrovia Daily News Post* of September 9, 1940, he had been a gold miner in Alaska since 1911. By 1918 he is working as a laborer for the Yukon Gold Company in Flat City, Alaska. In 1920 public records show him a prospector along Otter Creek. It is unclear if he and Nellie lived for a time in Huntingburg, Indiana since he is listed in an Evansville, Indiana newspaper as a former resident of the town. See the *Evansville Press*, September 11, 1940.

[119] McNeil Island Penitentiary, Photos and Records of Prisoners Received, 1887-1939, accessed via Ancestry.com.
[120] Federal census record, 1930. Gilley Bates married Emma Foss Holmstead on November 8, 1913 in Fairbanks, Alaska adopting her daughter Myrtle from an earlier marriage to Fred Holmstead. Emma died on February 4, 1920 in Stanwood and indeed was reported in ill health by the *Iditarod Pioneer* in August of 1917 causing them to journey back to Stanwood from Otter Creek. Gilbert is actually listed twice in the 1930 federal census. Besides logging in Mason County, he is also shown living with his new in-laws the Munsons in Stanwood. Their property lay just north to that owned by Billy and Samuel Bates. Gilbert married Levine Munson on January 4, 1930 in Pierce County, Washington. See federal census data from 1910 and 1930 and Washington marriage certificate for the marriage of Gilbert and Levine. The obituary of Alex Bates said that one of his first jobs was as an engineer on a steamboat and he gave that up to mine in the Yukon. However, Alex's name is not mentioned in press accounts as a member of Bates Bros. mining company. Following his Klondike experience, it is reported that Alex spent the rest of his life, for the most part, logging around the Puget Sound; Alex, Gilbert and Billy's wives are identified as living in Shelton when their attendance is listed at the 84th birthday party for the Bates brothers' mother Marie. See the *Stanwood News*, August 13, 1925.
[121] Mercedes Rogers Bates was born in Arlington on June 5, 1891 to Leonidust Rogers (1838 – 1925) and Georgia Ann Anderson Rogers (1870 – 1958). Samuel and Mercedes Bates had four sons: Robert Mooney Bates (1913 -1992), Samuel Linsey Bates (1914 – 1937), David R. Bates (1917 – 1937) and George Louis Bates (1920 – 1958). Obituary files of the Stanwood Area Historical Society; Ancestry.com.
[122] Essex, *The Stanwood Story*, vol. 1, p. 16.
[123] Essex, *The Stanwood Story*, vol. 1, p. 25-26; *Tacoma Daily Ledger*, December 13, 1905.
[124] *Tacoma Daily Ledger*, September 13, 1908.
[125] Essex, *The Stanwood Story*, vol. 1, p. 25.
[126] *Seattle Daily Times*, July 14, 1907.
[127] *The Ranch* (Seattle, WA), November 15, 1907.
[128] *Seattle Daily Times*, July 14, 1907.
[129] *Seattle Daily Times*, May 10, 1912.

Bibliography

Books:

Pierre Berton, *The Klondike Fever: The Life and Death of the Last Great Gold Rush,* (Auckland, New Zealand: Pickle Partners Publishing, 2015).

Howard, Blum, *The Floor of Heaven: A True Tale of the Last Frontier and the Yukon Gold Rush* (New York City: Crown Publishing, 2012).

William Whitfield, *History of Snohomish County,* vol. II, (Chicago, Seattle: Pioneer Publishing Company, 1926).

Charlene Porsild, *Gamblers and Dreamers: Women, Men and Community in the Klondike* (Chicago: University of Chicago Press, 1999)

Alice Essex, *The Stanwood Story,* vol. I (Stanwood, WA: Stanwood Camano News, 1997).

Thomas Ostenson Stine, Scandinavians on the Pacific, Puget Sound, (Project Gutenberg: [EBook #42384], March 21, 2013).

Agnes Deans Cameron, *The New North: Being Some Account of a Woman's Journey through Canada to the Arctic* (Project Gutenberg: [EBook #12874], July 10, 2004).

David M. Buerge, Peter Henning, Jr. (ed.), *The Builder: The Life of Peter Henning, 1868-1955, privately printed.*

An Illustrated History of Skagit and Snohomish Counties, Their People, Their Commerce and Their Resources, (Interstate Publishing Company, 1906).

Outlaw Tales of the Old West: Fifty True Stories of Desperadoes, Crooks, Criminals, and Bandits, Erin Turner (ed.) (Guilford, CT and Helena Montana, TWODOT, 2016).

J. H. Macdonnell, *Sketches Illustrating the Early Settlement and History of Glengarry in Canada,* (Montreal: W. Foster Brown & Co., 1893).

Gregg Olsen, *Starvation Heights* (New York: Three Rivers Press, 1997).

Jan Olof G. Lindström and Karen L. Olson, *The Platinum King: Andrew Olson's Story,* (Bothell, WA: Book Publishers Network, 2004).

The Klondike's "Dear Little Nuggett," Ian Macdonald and Betty O'Keefe (eds.) (Victoria, B.C.: Horsdal & Schubart,1996).

Websites/Digital Media

The Emigration from Sweden to the USA, Swedish History - Hans Högman (hhogman.se).

R.J. Roan, Before the Klondike there was Forty Mile - North of 60 Mining News (miningnewsnorth.com)

The "Golden Staircase," University of Washington, Chilkoot Pass: The "Golden Staircase" — UW Libraries (washington.edu)

J. Kingston Pierce, "Panic of 1893, Seattle's First Great Depression," Essay 2030, Historylink.org, November 24, 1999, Panic of 1893: Seattle's First Great Depression - HistoryLink.org

Joe Carroll Marsh, Biography: 0004 - Published: July 2014 - #PWHS (prowrestlinghistoricalsociety.com)

Gold Discovered in the Yukon - HISTORY

Area History — Gold Fever Prospecting (goldfeveralaska.com)

Bess Lovejoy, SmithsonianMag.com, October 28, 2014

The Doctor Who Starved Her Patients to Death | History | Smithsonian Magazine

"Dredgery": Researching the Life and Times of Canadian Number Four, *Archivaria*, Journal of the Association of Canadian Archivists, #22, (Summer, 1986), "Dredgery": Researching the Life and Times of Canadian Number Four | Archivaria.

"Hazzard, Linda Barfield (1867-1938), Historylink.org, Essay 7955

Photographers of Fargo, N.D., Institute for Regional Studies, North Dakota State University, Fargo, 2001. Accessed September 4, 2021. Untitled Document (ndsu.edu).

Chilkoot Pass: The "Golden Staircase," University of Washington, Chilkoot Pass: The "Golden Staircase" — UW Libraries (washington.edu)

"Hydro Power in Southeast Intrigues Leaders," August 25, 2007, available digitally at Alaska Journal | Hydro power in Southeast intrigues leaders

"Town of Chinik, now known as Golovin," historical notes, University of Washington, digital collections, Town of Chinik, now known as Golovin - Alaska,

Western Canada and United States - University of Washington Digital Collections

J. Kingston Pierce, "Panic of 1893, Seattle's First Great Depression," Essay 2030, Historylink.org, November 24, 1999, Panic of 1893: Seattle's First Great Depression - HistoryLink.org

National Park Service, "Series: Chilkoot Tramways," Series: Chilkoot Tramways (nps.gov)

Charles Hawley and Karen Olson, "Anders Olof Olsson: Andrew Olson, (1885-1981)," 2005, Andrew Olson (alaskamininghalloffame.org)

Sarah Hurst, *North of 60 Mining News*, January 30, 2005, 'The Platinum King: Andrew Olson's Story' - North of 60 Mining News (miningnewsnorth.com)

Arthur V. Buel - Biography of a Nevada Caricaturist | ONE (onlinenevada.org)

Biography: 0004 - Published: July 2014 - #PWHS (prowrestlinghistoricalsociety.com)

Frank 'Paddy' Slavin: The 'Sydney Cornstalk' – Yukon News (yukon-news.com).

Journal of Combative Sport: Gotch in Talk of Dawson (ejmas.com)

Alaska Mining Hall of Fame Inductees - John Beaton

Lars Ostnes (alaskamininghalloffame.org)

BLM-Alaska Open File Report 66, Library_Alaska_OpenFileReport66.pdf (blm.gov).

Boxrec.com

Black Sheep of Alaska, alaskaweb.org/blacksheep/index.html

John Waters, Stampede: Gold Fever and Disaster in the Klondike | RealClearDefense

North of 60 Mining News, accessed August 20, 2021, Before the Klondike there was Forty Mile - North of 60 Mining News (miningnewsnorth.com).

The Emigration from Sweden to the USA, Swedish History - Hans Högman (hhogman.se).

Andrew Olson (alaskamininghalloffame.org).

Hewitt and Jimmy Wheeler, Biography: 0004 - Published: July 2014 - #PWHS (prowrestlinghistoricalsociety.com).

Flat and Iditarod Oral History Interviews, 1993-1995, BLM-Alaska Open File Report 66, Library_Alaska_OpenFileReport66.pdf (blm.gov)

Journal of Combative Sport: Gotch in Talk of Dawson (ejmas.com),

Photographers of Fargo, N.D., Institute for Regional Studies, North Dakota State University, Fargo, 2001. Accessed September 4, 2021. Untitled Document (ndsu.edu).

Alaska Journal of Commerce (August 2007), "Hydro Power in Southeast Intrigues Leaders," August 25, 2007, available digitally at Alaska Journal | Hydro power in Southeast intrigues leaders.

Archie Binns from his book *Northwest Gateway*, quoted by Pierce in *Columbia*, *The Magazine of Northwest History*, (Winter 1993-94): Vol. 7, No. 42. Panic of 1893.pdf.

WrestlingClassics.com Message Board: Gotch in the Klondike

Darrell Hookey, Boxing in the Klondike - The Klondike Weekly (yukonalaska.com)

Yukon News – Yukon News (yukon-news.com)

Home (boxingbiographies.co.uk)

Mike Chapman on Frank Gotch - YouTube

The Cyber Boxing Zone

U.S. GEOLOGICAL SURVEY B ULLETIN 2125, GOLD PLACERS OF THE HISTORICAL FORTYMILE RIVER REGION, ALASKA, 1996-- report.pdf (usgs.gov).

Frank Gotch Wrestling History (legacyofwrestling.com)

Terrie Hanke, "Eye on the Trail: Iditarod and Flat @ Mile 432," January 23, 2021, Eye on the Trail: Iditarod and Flat @ Mile 432 – Iditarod

Newspapers/Periodicals

Seattle Post-Intelligencer

Seattle Daily Times

Stanwood Tidings

Stanwood News

Twin City News

Daily Morning Alaskan

Daily Alaska Dispatch

Washington Standard

Everett Herald

Klondike Nugget (Dawson City, Yukon, Terr.)

Tacoma Daily Ledger

Tacoma News Tribune

Tacoma Daily News

Alaska Journal of Commerce

San Francisco Examiner

San Francisco Call Bulletin

Yukon News (Whitehorse, Yukon, Canada)

The Register, (Adelaide, South Australia

Oregon Journal (Portland, OR)

Daily Morning Alaskan (Skagway, AK)

Waterbury Evening Democrat (CT)

Baltimore Sun

Duluth New-Tribune

Spokane Herald

Topeka State Journal

Baltimore American

Columbus [Ohio] *Dispatch*

Fairbanks Daily Times

Fairbanks Daily News-Miner

Iditarod Pioneer

Seward Gateway

Anchorage Daily Times

Alaska Daily Empire

Kusko Times (Takotna, AK)

Juneau Empire

Stanwood News

The Herald (Jasper, Indiana)

Evansville Press (Indiana)

Douglas Island News (Douglas, AK)

The Glengarry News

Ottumwa (IA) *Semi-Weekly*

Daily Nonpareil (Council Bluffs, IA)

Decorah (IA) *Public Opinion,*

Minneapolis Journal,

Evening-Times Republican (Marshalltown, IA)

Chicago Tribune

Douglas Island News

Daily Ardmore (OK Terr.)

Daily People (NY City)

Jackson Citizen Patriot (Jackson, MI)

San Diego Union

Omaha Daily Bee

Oregon Journal (Portland, OR)

Washington Times (Washington, D.C.)

Quad City Times (Davenport, IA)

Spokane Chronicle

Twin City News (Stanwood, WA)

Salt Lake Herald

Sacramento Bee

Evening Star (Washington, D.C.)

Fairbanks Daily News Miner

Trenton Daily Times (Trenton, NJ)

The Province (Vancouver, B.C.)

Columbus Dispatch

Boston Globe

Buffalo Morning Express

Wilkes Barre Times (Wilkes Barre, PA)

Duluth News-Tribune (Duluth, MN)

Waterbury Evening Democrat (Waterbury CT)

Topeka State Journal

Nevada State Journal (Reno, NV)

Douglas Daily Dispatch (Douglas, AZ)

Monrovia Daily News Post (CA)

San Francisco Chronicle

Index

C

About The Author

Born and raised in the Midwest, Richard Hanks came of age in Southern California where he worked as a journalist, curator, archivist, professor, editor and author. His academic fields of interest include 19th and 20th century American history with particular focus on Native American history for which he earned his PhD at the University of California, Riverside. Upon retiring in 2013 he moved to Camano Island, Washington where he volunteered at the Hibulb Cultural Center on the Tulalip Reservation and as a writer and researcher for the Stanwood Area Historical Society. He was president of the Society from January 2017 to December 2020. He and his wife Robin also began Coyote Hill Press in 2013. His other books are *The Harris Company* (co-author), Arcadia Press, 2008; *This War is for a Whole Life: The Culture of Resistance Among Southern California Indians, 1850-1866*, Ushkana Press, 2012; *Vermont's Proper Son: The Letters of Soldier and Scholar, Edwin Hall Higley, 1861-1871*,Coyote Hill Press, 2014; *A Living History of the Soboba Band of Luiseño Indians and their Connections to the San Jacinto Valley* (co-author), Soboba Cultural Resource Department, 2018; *Solemn The Drums Thrill: Essays on the Fallen Heroes of Stanwood Camano--World War I to Afghanistan,* Coyote Hill Press, 2020. In 2021 he released his first novel, *Gentle Presence: One Woman's Journey Through Faith,* Coyote Hill Press.

Richard in Seattle, WA in front of the Arthur Foss, built in 1889 as Wallowa at Portland, OR and is likely the oldest wooden tugboat afloat in the world.

COYOTE HILL PRESS

Made in the USA
Columbia, SC
03 March 2023